Making a Difference

Making a Difference

Instructional Leadership That Drives Self-Reflection and Values the Expertise of Teachers

Ian M. Mette
Dwayne Ray Cormier
Yanira Oliveras

ROWMAN & LITTLEFIELD
Lanham • Boulder • New York • London

Published by Rowman & Littlefield
An imprint of The Rowman & Littlefield Publishing Group, Inc.
4501 Forbes Boulevard, Suite 200, Lanham, Maryland 20706
www.rowman.com

86-90 Paul Street, London EC2A 4NE, United Kingdom

British Library Cataloguing in Publication Information Available

Library of Congress Cataloging-in-Publication Data

Names: Mette, Ian M., author. | Cormier, Dwayne Ray, 1980– author. | Oliveras, Yanira,
    1972– author.
Title: Making a difference : instructional leadership that drives self-reflection and values
    the expertise of teachers / Ian M. Mette, Dwayne Ray Cormier, Yanira Oliveras.
Description: Lanham, Maryland : Rowman & Littlefield, 2023. | Includes bibliographical
    references. | Summary: "Supervision frameworks tend to lack the ability to identify,
    address, and provide feedback about how racial, cultural, and socioeconomic factors
    contribute to the sociocultural gap that so often exists between teachers and students
    in the US. To accomplish this, however, a more culturally responsive system of
    instructional feedback will need to support educators to consider how students who
    are minoritized, marginalized, and otherized in the US see themselves as belonging to
    a democratic US society"— Provided by publisher.
Identifiers: LCCN 2023023998 (print) | LCCN 2023023999 (ebook) | ISBN
    9781475872255 (cloth) | ISBN 9781475872262 (paperback) | ISBN
    9781475872279 (epub)
Subjects: LCSH: Educational equalization—United States. | Culturally relevant
    pedagogy—United States. | Minorities—Education—United States. | Educational
    leadership—United States.
Classification: LCC LC213.2 .M47 2023 (print) | LCC LC213.2 (ebook) | DDC
    379.2/60973—dc23/eng/20230718
LC record available at https://lccn.loc.gov/2023023998
LC ebook record available at https://lccn.loc.gov/2023023999

This book is dedicated to educators who believe that—together—we can make a more equitable society for all children in the United States. This book is especially for those who dream, resist, unlearn and relearn, and form coalitions of educators who care about creating a more just and inclusive society.

Ian M. Mette
September 2023
Dwayne Ray Cormier
September 2023
Yanira Oliveras
September 2023

Contents

Preface

Since President Obama left office in 2016, politics centering on whiteness in the United States have been used to ratify policies that deliberately hinder teaching historical truths (e.g., US slavery), resulting in the ongoing oppression of racially and culturally marginalized groups. American society has transformed into a cultural battleground for educators, students, and families inside and outside of PK–12 classrooms. US education has become an "us versus them" arena in which politics are being played out. Politicians are engaging in rhetoric about widespread voter fraud, dictating what educators can and cannot teach, and promoting White supremacist ideologies (i.e., whiteness) as the population becomes more racially and culturally diverse.

During this time period, the United States has seen a dramatic rise in racialized violence, control over women's reproductive rights, and xenophobic policies that seek to separate children from their parents. Worse yet are the policies, of which there are many on the books and more pending, that codify conservative, White supremacist ideologies preventing the teaching of historical accuracies about our racialized society that influence social outcomes to this day. Social dominance based on various sociocultural identities—including race, ethnicity, gender, class, orientation/identity, ability, and other lived experiences—are alive and well in the United States.

In this book, we aim to illustrate how education, as a system, contributes to historical inequities that exist and are perpetuated throughout US society. One of the quickest ways to contribute to a more progressive, equitable, and inclusive society is to change what is taught, how it is taught, and for whom it is intended. However, making this shift will require coalitions of people—similar to what Fred Hampton suggested—to come together and relate to one another, to rethink, reimagine, and reconceptualize what the US educational system should look like and be like in practice.

It is in this spirit that we write this book. As a Black male (Dwayne), a Latina (Yanira), and a White male (Ian), we experience education differently through our own experiences and identities. We also believe that we can come together, as educators, to make a more equitable, inclusive, and representative society. However, we can only do so if we are intentional and strategic with our policies and practices. In this spirit, we present this book to practitioners so that you might consider how to address the social, racial, and economic inequities in your school community.

Introduction

We wrote this book, *Making a Difference: Instructional Leadership That Drives Self-Reflection and Values the Expertise of Teachers*, in the hope of providing a framework to discuss how education, as a system, can address the historical inequities that are perpetuated throughout US society. To be clear, we want to acknowledge that it is not a lockstep process, and that this is simply a guide—a roadmap of sorts—to help practitioners develop more equitable outcomes for students through culturally responsive teaching practices. That said, we believe this paradigm shift is desperately needed if US society is to ever move past its oppressive and violent foundation.

We start with the idea of the instructional leader being an equity leader. Chapter 1 asks educators to (re)consider to whom and to what are we most accountable, and to challenge the notion that education exists to produce test scores and contribute to a global economic engine. Instead, we provide a foundation for educational leaders to reexamine why we need to engage in culturally responsive instruction, and why it is critical for instructional supervisors to shift their paradigms and practices away from privileged identities and perspectives. Through this work, educators can develop empathy for students experiencing marginalization and othering.

In part I, we address the feedback loop problem in US schools. Chapter 2 discusses how we can shift feedback from hierarchical perspectives that privilege power and move away from evaluation practices that exist to control students and teachers. Chapter 3 explores how we can liberate ourselves from prepackaged curriculum and teacher evaluation systems to create feedback that is culturally responsive and useful in generating more equitable outcomes. Chapter 4 provides a framework for developing a community of culturally responsive instructors (CCRI) that value acts of educational resistance and address systemic inequities.

In part II, we discuss the value of a representative team of instructional leaders. Chapter 5 explains why we must be intentional about representation when providing feedback about instruction, specifically the importance of diverse sociocultural perspectives providing feedback. Chapter 6 outlines what culturally responsive instructional supervision looks like and how data can be collected through walkthroughs and analyzed to determine future professional development efforts. Chapter 7 establishes what should happen when instruction is observed not to be inclusive, and how developmental feedback can eventually lead to cultural proficiency.

In part III, we ask practitioners to consider the supports and structures needed for developing culturally responsive instruction through supervision. Chapter 8 discusses why growth must start with the self and how agency and expertise can be leveraged to develop more culturally responsive instructional instruction. Chapter 9 raises the importance of growing with critical colleagues and how group learning is an opportunity to discuss equity and drive growth. Chapter 10 provides an outline of how to use peer-led classroom observations to drive equitable outcomes across a school building and to deconstruct systems of inequity.

We believe this book will be useful to practitioners in that it provides a framework to resist the technorational approaches to school reform that have been in place since the inception of NCLB. Through the practice of culturally responsive instructional supervision, we believe schools can transform from systems of oppression to systems of opportunity. However, we must shift the idea that feedback is hierarchical, and we must stop believing that feedback is bad. Feedback is good, but only if it is used for good causes. It is in this vein that we present this book and hope that through feedback about culturally responsive instruction all students can experience an equitable education.

Chapter 1

The Instructional Leader as an Equity Leader

We believe that education, as a system, can contribute to addressing the historical inequities that exist and are perpetuated throughout US society. In this book, you will read the authors' unabashed attempt to resist the ongoing implementation of the accountability experiment stemming from the Nation at Risk report commissioned by the US Department of Education during the Reagan administration. The report's scope was broadened with the introduction of Goals 2000 during the Clinton administration. It was further solidified with the No Child Left Behind (NCLB) legislation passed during the Bush administration.

To be clear, we believe that accountability is good—if aimed at addressing the inequities that exist within various marginalized and othered groups and individuals in the United States. However, history has shown that the pursuit of increased test scores is fraught with peril. Specifically, the hyperfocus on test scores has allowed for the infiltration of corporate interests in pursuit of profiting from labeling children as successful or failures, and this has proven disastrous and destructive for children from historically marginalized racial, ethnic, and economic backgrounds.

If the US education system is ever to address the inequities that exist along racial, ethnic, and socioeconomic lines, we must develop coalitions of educators who are able to tackle, head-on, the inequalities experienced by students, parents, and community members that are minoritized, marginalized, and otherized in US society. The only way to accomplish this lofty goal is to rethink, reimagine, and (re)envision a system that addresses how teachers think about instruction and how students internalize instruction in classrooms across the United States.

As Milner IV[1] suggests, educators do not need to be of the same racial or cultural group to contribute to a more equitable educational system. However, educators must recognize how US society was socially constructed, with

1

whiteness at its center, and how historical inequities along these lines continue to be perpetuated in the education system. Furthermore, educators must have a thorough understanding of how their sociocultural construction can either contribute to or impede their ability to honor and value their students' diverse cultural and lived experiences. Keeping this in mind, we present this book as a framework to help educators address these challenges and create a more empowering and inclusive instructional experience for all children in the United States.

TO WHOM AND WHAT ARE WE MOST ACCOUNTABLE?

To unpack the work that must be done for our education system to move forward, we must first address the recent history of the US public education system and how top-down policies heavily influence educational and student outcomes. There is an entire generation of educators, paraprofessionals, teachers, and administrators that have only known the high-stakes accountability structure that started with NCLB in 2001. During this time, educators have been told by wealthy, mostly White, policymakers that to be a successful education system we must create student outcomes measured almost exclusively by producing high test scores on standardized tests.

Even when President Obama had the chance to move away from these types of metrics, his administration continued with these policy measures with the Every Student Succeeds Act (ESSA) in 2015. During these twenty years of policy enactments, schools and the students they serve have been labeled as at-risk, dangerous, and chronically failing *due to the instruction occurring within schools*. What has happened, as a result, is the misrepresentation of student ability that perpetuates a deficit narrative about communities, almost always which is directly correlated with race, ethnicity, and socioeconomic status (SES), among other identities.

Policies used by the United States since 2001 have perpetuated damaging narratives about historically racially marginalized students and parents, reinforcing the idea that these students are either unwilling to learn, unable to learn, or undeserving of quality education.[2] Perhaps most nefarious, these policies have helped to create an enormous industry of prepackaged curricula, aligned directly to high-stakes tests, that serve the economic interests of large corporations and prop up ideologies that are anti-Black, reinforce whiteness as the norm, and lack any sort of sociocultural understanding of how to create equitable instructional opportunities.[3]

If you were to ask most educators in the United States why they went into education, almost none of them would say it is because they want to perpetuate the inequities in our society or support an education industry that is valued at over $600 billion a year.[4] Almost all of them would say they entered education to help make a difference in the lives of students because of their love for teaching students to understand more about who they are and how they might make a difference in the world and because they truly love working with children.

However, schools' ability to meet children's individual needs has decreased year after year, resulting in an education crisis. Consequently, many teachers leave the classroom because they lack the necessary professional development, skills, and tools to teach all children effectively and achieve positive societal outcomes.[5] For the education system to address the historical inequities within our society, we must stop subjecting ourselves to accountability measures, such as test scores, that primarily focus on economic outcomes.

Measuring teaching effectiveness and student success based solely on economic output and job opportunities is an impractical and narrow-minded approach. Instead, we need to focus on more comprehensive accountability measures considering a wider range of factors (e.g., quality of teacher preparation and school resources).

Educators must start reengaging with the belief that we are accountable for addressing the historical inequities in the United States since its inception. However, educators can only do so much within their classrooms without school administrators' support and adequate resources. Subsequently, teacher leaders, principals, and central office administrators must look to research-based practices such as culturally responsive instruction, a theoretical and practical framework in which instructional leaders provide formative feedback—the supervision of instruction.

WHY LEADERSHIP IS CRUCIAL TO THE CONVERSATION

To address the documented social and racial inequities that are continually propagated through US school systems, educators must make the shift from deficit ideologies that are grounded in economic accountability structures and shift toward use of asset-based pedagogies[6] as an act of resistance and transformation. In doing so, educators can accomplish the ultimate form of accountability, which is being responsive to and honoring the cultural assets *students and parents bring to schools and classrooms*. However, this change requires leadership to alter messages, practices, and policies about what student success looks like as a result of culturally appropriate and responsive instructional practices.

To accomplish this change in how we actualize culturally responsive instruction in the classroom, specifically what this kind of teaching looks like in classrooms across the schoolhouse, requires leadership that values feedback *about* instruction. This feedback should value vulnerability, understand and address the sociocultural gaps across education in the United States, and celebrate taking risks that bring us away from teaching to the test and empower children to see themselves represented in their education.

However, feedback cannot be a continuation of the high-stakes accountability movement that values evaluating teachers by placing them on a one through four continuum that determines their worth as an instructor. Instead, the feedback must be formative and supportive in nature. Educational leaders—teachers, principals, and central office administrators—must remove "getting into trouble" from feedback about observed instruction in a classroom and pivot toward a system of support that values "getting into good trouble" that encourages teachers to think critically about how their instruction can help make the United States a more equitable and just society.

At the core of this work is a fundamental shift in philosophy about how teachers learn best as adults. Throughout the US education accountability experiment, educators have increasingly experienced technocratic attempts to measure teacher effectiveness, which have placed power in the hands of administrators to assess teachers, most notably based on their ability to produce results on standardized tests.[7] To make this change in philosophy requires placing less emphasis on "scientific" measurement supported by teacher evaluation programs like Marzano and Danielson and instead necessitates honoring the development of teachers as *adult learners*.

Historically, this type of work has been supported through instructional supervision literature, which posits that through formative feedback a supervisor can help a teacher identify areas of strength and opportunities for improvement, as well as select individualized professional development opportunities, all of which ultimately leads to improved instruction.[8] Supervision—providing formative feedback to support the development of reflective stances about instruction—is a core function of school leadership and instructional leadership more specifically.

Supervision is designed to engage teachers in driving their own learning and professional development to become more aware of how their instruction is experienced by students, as well as how learning is applied in meaningful ways from the perspective of students. As such, it focuses on treating educators as professionals who, with ongoing and targeted support, can continually develop throughout their career and continually increase educational outcomes for students. However, supervision—at least traditionally—is problematic in that it places an enormous amount of hierarchical power in the hands of the principal in determining what quality instruction looks like.

Supervision frameworks also lack the ability to identify, address, and provide feedback about how racial, cultural, and socioeconomic factors contribute to the sociocultural gap that so often exists between teachers and students in the United States.[9] It has often masqueraded as "clinical," suggesting it is somehow an objective practice that neither needs to account for positionality and identity in how feedback is provided from a supervisor, nor does it need to consider how feedback is perceived from the perspective of a teacher.

Supervision, one of the core competencies developed in almost every master's-level educational leadership program in the United States, has remained ahistorical, apolitical, and often colorblind in its conceptions and frameworks of how feedback is provided about instruction.[10] As such, supervision has perpetuated the inequitable and nonrepresentative educational experiences in the United States. Given this reality, we must rethink supervision practices to address the immoral actions and beliefs that supported enslavement, colonization of an entire continent, and gender bias that prevented the voting rights of women, all of which are examples of beliefs that permeate modern US society.

WHY WE NEED CULTURALLY RESPONSIVE INSTRUCTIONAL SUPERVISION NOW

If, as educators, we are ever to contribute to addressing the historic inequities within our society, we must learn to work together, through broad coalitions, to make the US education system more equitable and inclusive. To accomplish this lofty goal is no easy task. It cannot be accomplished through a standardization of education—that is abundantly clear through the failed efforts that started with NCLB and have lasted for over twenty years.

A more culturally responsive system of instruction can, however, be accomplished through the development of educators who are aware of how their instruction is internalized, specifically how it is perceived. It also requires educators to consider what perspectives are allowed to be centered within the classroom and the curriculum, as well as how it empowers students who are minoritized, marginalized, and otherized in the United States to see themselves as part of a society that is truly democratic. And it requires professional development to use feedback as a vehicle for dialogue about where our country has come, where it is currently, and where it will go next.

Given where we are, racially and sociopolitically, in US society, school systems can no longer ignore the importance of feedback about instruction. Achievement of some students, typically White and almost always those from middle- or upper-class backgrounds, and failure for others, those from historically marginalized groups, only serve to support troupes about groups of people.

Based on this history and lived reality, we believe our country has two options: continue with how we have always approached education, which benefits those who belong to dominant identities (White, male, middle-to-upper class, heterosexual, etc.), or engage in the work to develop a deep understanding of why sociocultural gaps exist in the first place and then provide professional development and tools for mitigating educational sociocultural gaps. This will require our profession to take a hard look in the mirror to make changes on a systemic level, including educators being willing to question the benefits of whiteness and a middle-class existence openly.

It will also require teachers to actively critique how education practices and policies reinforce various aspects of privilege, reinforce anti-Black approaches to education, and lack cultural competence more broadly.[11] Perhaps of most importance, this work must ask the question: what does achievement matter if US schools and society remain inequitable?

HOW DEVELOPING EMPATHY CAN
MAKE OUR COMMUNITIES BETTER

Given that 80 percent of teachers and administrators in the United States are White,[12] there is a huge need to develop educators' capacity and desire to reflect on their own sociocultural construction and cultural competence. This requires educators to not only be self-reflective and examine their own identities, but to also develop a deeper understanding of how they perceive sociocultural constructions related to race, gender, ethnicity, SES, ability, spatiality, and lived experiences, among other aspects of identity.[13] As such, the ability to be critically conscious about the lived experiences of students and parents who come from historically marginalized groups is essential to closing opportunity gaps.

This shift—an increase in cultural competence of the lived experiences of all students—can only be accomplished through ongoing support and reflection about what is observed in the classroom; it is not something that can just be learned in a graduate-level class or professional development. From an adult learning perspective, cultural competence can be developed through feedback that centers on lived experiences related to racial, cultural, and economic inequities and differences.[14] Through culturally responsive instructional supervision, these tasks can help teachers reflect on their cultural competence and contribute to a more just education system.

To address these instructional blind spots that exist within all educators, we believe a radical shift must take place in how we think about providing feedback about instruction. Regardless of positionality or identity, we all have taken for granted assumptions that surface and resurface throughout our teaching—and we believe that with the right type of structure and support, anyone can become more culturally responsive and competent. However, teachers must be willing to do the work *and* have their assumptions questioned about how our society and sociocultural identities are constructed.

Throughout this book we will discuss what we see as the systemic and cognitive obstacles to providing feedback that can lead to more vulnerable reflection about sociocultural gaps and how schools can become a community of reflective learners. We will also engage in structures that suggest why a principal should never be the sole provider of culturally responsive instructional supervision and how classroom observations can be used as data points to identify culturally responsive instruction.

Related, the framework we provide details what type of plan should be in place if and when teaching that lacks culturally responsive approaches is observed. We will also talk about shifting the idea of instructional supervision from the power of a principal to the responsibility of a teacher, which requires personal growth, the support of critical colleagues, and welcoming peer observations to help drive more equitable outcomes for students.

We will detail the feedback loop problem that is experienced throughout schools in the United States. Currently, there is a major problem with how feedback is provided in US school systems, specifically the hyperfocus on evaluative measures that fail to treat teachers as professionals. Due to the incredibly intense high-stakes accountability experiment, feedback about instruction has become evaluative, fear-laden, and used to control how teachers teach and students learn.

To shift away from this damaging feedback paradigm, we offer our reflections on the purpose of instruction. Specifically, we engage with the idea that educators who apply culturally responsive instructional supervision must act as shepherds and guardians of inclusion. Through this paradigm shift, supervisors can reframe feedback to value relationships, cocreate knowledge, and promote accountability to create more inclusive instruction to increase students' sense of belonging and academic success.

LEARNING TO STAND UP TO HATRED

Before we delve into the core of the book, we would be remiss if we didn't share a bit of our own positionality for the reader, and why we think this matters in the context of what you are about to read. As a Black male (Dwayne), a Latina (Yanira), and a White male (Ian), we experience education through our own lenses, identities, experiences, roles, and regions of the United States.

We come together as committed educators who believe that education in the United States can benefit all children—if we are intentional about how we address social, racial, and economic inequities that exist throughout the US education system.

Through this book, we hope to provide a framework that empowers *you*. As an educational leader in your school, we hope you are someone who wants to contribute to "a radical moral imagination"[15] that sheds whiteness, White supremacy, and contributes to the liberation of all children—Black, Brown, Indigenous, Asian, White, and other—from our history of violence, oppression, and wide-ranging forms of discrimination. But make no mistake about it; if these efforts are to be successful you will need to develop committed coalitions of people who are able and willing to fight for equity and inclusion.

Establishing and implementing culturally responsive instructional supervision will require classrooms to be deprivatized and collaborative efforts be developed to provide feedback that directly addresses the political and moral actions that promote White supremacy, gender discrimination, ethnic discrimination, and gender bias, among others, from the inception of the United States up to the present. It will also require acknowledging how these various sociocultural gaps can be addressed and remediated in US schools, but only when we openly discuss how our various identities interact with what we teach, how we teach, and how our teaching is perceived.

Throughout this work, educators will face various barriers, including state bans on addressing historical inequities, politically mobilized school board members, and parents of students who protest that learning about the historically marginalized is not appropriate for their child. And yet the children of the United States deserve nothing less than to have the opportunity to learn the truth about how our country was founded and what that means for where we are currently as a society.

We believe that through culturally responsive instructional supervision, and a focus on instructional practices that allow students to contribute to a more just, equitable, and peaceful world, educators might be able to support a more democratic society and a truly representative country. We envision an education system that is unafraid to stand up to bigotry and hatred. It is with this challenge that we offer you our book, which we present in support and in solidarity.

NOTES

1. Milner IV, H. R. (2007). Race, culture, and researcher positionality: Working through dangers seen, unseen, and unforeseen. *Educational Researcher, 36*(7), 388–400.

2. Givens, J. (2021). *Fugitive pedagogy: Carter G. Woodson and the art of Black teaching*. Harvard University Press.

3. Cormier, D. R. (2021). Assessing preservice teachers' cultural competence with the cultural proficiency continuum q-sort. *Educational Researcher, 50*(1), 17–29.

4. National Center for Education Statistics (NCES). (2017). *2017 Digest of Education Statistics*. https://nces.ed.gov/programs/digest/d16/tables/dt16_236.10.asp?current=yes

5. ASCD. (2019). Confronting the crisis of educational inequity. *Educational Leadership, 14*(23). https://www.ascd.org/el/articles/confronting-the-crisis-of-education-inequity

6. Khalifa, M. (2020). *Culturally responsive school leadership* (4th ed.). Harvard Education Press; Muhammad, G. (2020). *Cultivating genius: An equity framework for culturally and historically responsive literacy*. Scholastic.

7. Mette, I. M., Aguilar, I., & Wieczorek, D. (2020). A thirty state analysis of teacher supervision and evaluation systems in the ESSA era. *Journal of Educational Supervision, 3*(2), 105–135.

8. Glickman, C. D., Gordon, S. P., & Ross-Gordon, J. M. (2018). *Supervision and instructional leadership: A developmental approach* (10th ed.). Pearson; and Zepeda, S. J. (2016). *Instructional supervision: Applying tools and concepts* (4th ed.). Routledge.

9. Cormier, D. R. (2022). Prototyping the Cultural Proficiency Continuum Dialogic Protocol with professional development school teacher interns. *Urban Education*. https://doi.org/10.1177/00420859221140405; Guerra, P. L., Baker, A. M., & Cotman, A. (2022). Instructional supervision: Is it culturally responsive? A textbook analysis. *Journal of Educational Supervision, 5*(1), 1–26. https://doi.org/10.31045/jes.5.1.1

10. Cormier, D. R., & Pandey, T. (2021). Semiotic analysis of a foundational textbook used widely across educational supervision. *Journal of Educational Supervision, 4*(2), 101–132.

11. Cormier, D. R. (2022). Prototyping the Cultural Proficiency Continuum Dialogic Protocol with professional development school teacher interns. *Urban Education*. https://doi.org/10.1177/00420859221140405

12. National Center for Education Statistics (NCES). (2016). Characteristics of public school teachers. https://nces.ed.gov/programs/coe/indicator_clr.asp

13. Fisher-Ari, T. R., Speights, R., Veazie, M., Haile, H., Tennies, E., & Ngo, H. (2020). Organizational cultural competence in PDS networks and teacher certification programs. In J. Ferrara, J. L. Nath, & R. S. Beebe, *Exploring cultural competence in professional development schools* (pp. 1–25). Information Age Publishing.

14. Cormier, D. R. (2022). Prototyping the Cultural Proficiency Continuum Dialogic Protocol with professional development school teacher interns. *Urban Education*. https://doi.org/10.1177/00420859221140405; Ladson-Billings, G. (2017). The (r)evolution will not be standardized. In D. Paris & H. S. Alim, *Culturally sustaining pedagogies: Teaching and learning for justice in a changing world* (pp. 141–156). Teachers College Press.

15. Laymon, K. (2018). *Heavy: An American memoir*. Scribner.

PART I

Addressing the Feedback Loop Problem in US Schools

Chapter 2

Shifting Feedback from Hierarchical to Helpful

Teacher evaluation—the primary method of receiving feedback about instructional practices in the United States—has been a huge part of the educational policy landscape since the inception of the high-stakes accountability movement. Further strengthened by ESSA, teacher evaluation systems often weigh a high percentage of teacher effectiveness, often upward of 50 percent of a teacher's evaluation, through the use of high-stakes test scores.[1]

While teacher evaluation (the summative feedback of performance over time) is useful to remove underperforming teachers from the classroom,[2] of which there certainly are some, there is little to no formal efforts to support teachers on a daily or weekly basis to reflect on instruction through formative feedback structures. What results is a feedback system used by policymakers to control the education profession with a variety of variables and technical levers that do nothing to improve the instructional practices of teachers, *and in fact contribute to* the widening of sociocultural and opportunity gaps in the United States.

Herein lies one of the major problems with the feedback loop in US schools. Feedback about instruction is intermittent, high stakes, and typically comes from a person of power—the principal. Occasionally, well-resourced schools employ an instructional coach to provide additional feedback in math and reading. However, these positions are almost always tied to content areas that are subjected to high-stakes testing and contribute to the devaluing of nontested subject areas that are deemed unworthy of additional instructional support.

Given these realities, feedback about instruction often is hierarchical, fails to incorporate feedback in subject areas that can address the societal foundations of historical inequities that exist in the United States, and is stressful due to the high-stakes nature of the feedback. It also places an inordinate amount of control in the hands of a principal, 80 percent of whom are White, to make decisions about the instructional needs of students and teachers in a school.

To be clear, we understand that teacher evaluation is a policy that is legally required. We understand that leaders cannot simply ignore a policy, mandate, or law. But we also believe that principals can and should rethink and reimagine the purpose of feedback, specifically how feedback about instruction can shift to constructive and helpful practice that occurs on a daily or weekly basis. Teacher evaluation—the practice of providing summative feedback about performance—is important. However, it should be used for human resource decisions when a teacher is unable to improve their performance after rounds of formative feedback.

The challenge is to consider how supervision—the practice of providing formative feedback to engage and empower teachers in improving their teaching practices—can be implemented in a way that supports teachers to develop reflective stances about instruction.[3] Furthermore, in the US society, which is heavily influenced by factors such as race, gender, ethnicity, socioeconomic status, ability, spatiality, and lived experiences, it is of critical importance for instructional leaders to be aware of how they provide formative feedback through instructional supervision, as well as the perceived usefulness and effectiveness of the provided feedback.

SHIFTING AWAY FROM PLANTATION PRACTICES

When we think about how feedback is provided to teachers about their performance, what most principals really engage in, knowingly or not, is a form of workplace behaviorism.[4] Through the US education system, principals apply their position of power and seek to control ideologies about the profession, as well as actively reinforce the values and beliefs of policymakers, most of which are aligned with testing scores. Figure 2.1 highlights this cycle, and what results are parallel structures that replicate plantation practices used to control the minds of teachers, as well as those of students and parents.

In education, this parallel structure results in a person of power (the principal, an overwhelming percentage of whom are White) controlling what is taught and who is considered high functioning (high test scores and funding models tied to achievement). If education is to help liberate our children from the violent and oppressive past, as well as address the present social inequities that exist within the United States, we must move past observation practices that attempt to constantly control the minds of teachers, students, and parents. Schools don't exist to control people—they are supposed to exist to educate a democratic society.

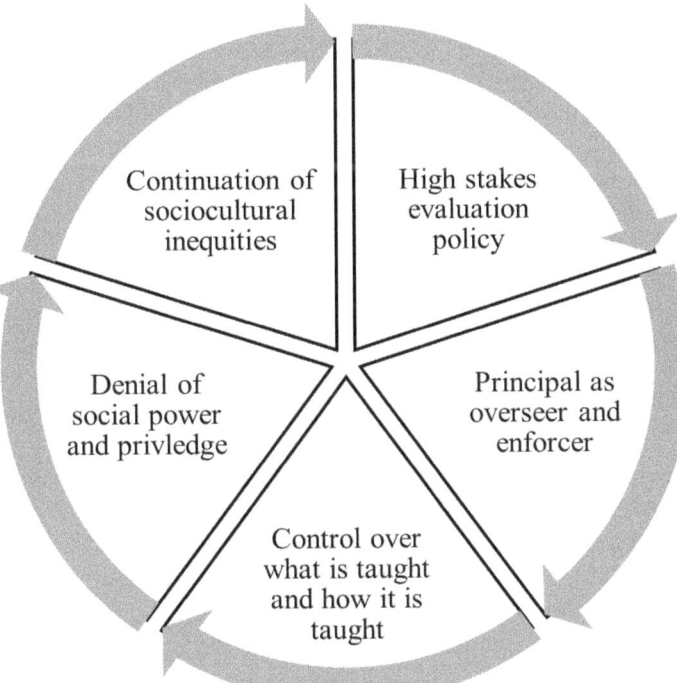

Figure 2.1.   Teacher Evaluation Contributing to Education as a System of Oppression

One of the main factors contributing to the idea of plantation practices through the system of teacher feedback is how race—but also ethnicity, gender, sexuality, and class, among other identities—contributes to our knowledge about education, specifically what is considered credible instruction.[5] Until the US public education system is willing to acknowledge most, if not all, educational policies benefit those with social power and privilege—typically middle-to-upper class White children—it is the responsibility of instructional leaders to continually address privileged sociocultural identities that influence educational practices.[6]

Unless educators in the field are willing to disrupt instructional practices that lack cultural responsiveness, education in the United States will remain a system of oppression, one that replicates plantation practices that seek to control what is taught, how it is taught, and who the instruction benefits. To be clear, none of us believe educators come to school every day attempting to engage in instruction that is culturally damaging. However, we all are part of an education *system*—one that is nefarious and increasingly one that actively resists equity-centered improvements.[7]

To contribute to socially just practices that address discriminatory policies and practices, educators must be willing to address the lived experiences of *all* students in the United States.[8] In many ways, we must actively fight against punitive teacher evaluation methods and instead create a system that supports vulnerability, examination of the historical context of US society, and ongoing feedback that is seen as supportive in aiding teacher reflection to become increasingly aware of the sociocultural gap.

Paulo Freire[9] suggests we must continually engage in the notion of problem-posing to improve the way we think about and engage in dialogue and pedagogy, and this is certainly true about supporting teachers to become more culturally proficient. To make this shift, however, we must empower teachers to take part in the co-construction of dialogue about instruction, specifically how it is implemented and impacts students who are minoritized, marginalized, and otherized.

The US education system will not change until we shift and transform how feedback is given about instruction, how teachers are empowered to implement instructional improvement efforts, and how educators can contribute to closing the sociocultural gap through repeated conversations and attempts. If formative feedback is to drive change, it must be culturally appropriate and responsive, and feedback about what is taught in the classroom must come from formative structures that define culturally responsive instructional supervision.

REEXAMINING THE PURPOSE OF
FEEDBACK ABOUT INSTRUCTION

To break away from plantation practices that seek to control aspects about what is taught and how it is taught, we must reexamine what we believe to be the purpose of giving feedback about instruction. There is a laundry list of things supervisors have been told are important to give feedback about, including but not limited to whether objectives are posted on the wall, the amount of technology being used, how behavior is managed, seating arrangements, assessment of student knowledge, among others.

What none of the templates, protocols, and continuums address, particularly the large-scale corporate frameworks such as Marzano and Danielson, is, *How and to what extent* does the instruction consider the lived experience of the student? None of the prepacked teacher evaluation systems help teachers reflect on their own cultural competence, and how or to what degree they take into account the way lessons are internalized by students who are minoritized, marginalized, or otherized. When we fail to develop a system that can support teachers to reflect upon sociocultural constructions and gaps, we not only fail our teachers, but we fail our students.

As educators, we are supposed to be *guardians of inclusion*. However, we cannot change the outcomes of the US education system until we change the way we think about instructional feedback. As highlighted in figure 2.2, our feedback should help teachers engage in reflection about racial, social, and economic injustices occurring throughout the United States and how their teaching might help students who are historically minoritized, marginalized, and otherized receive instruction that is more asset-based, anti-oppressive, and liberatory in nature. Feedback about instruction should support critical self-reflection about ways of knowing and how that translates (or not) to how students interpret and apply what is taught through instruction.

However, feedback about instruction should not make teachers feel bad about failing to list an objective on a wall. Instead, the feedback should be constructive and focus on helping teachers reflect on the level to which students were engaged and how and in what ways did they leverage their cultural competence to support the learning of *all* children. As instructional leaders—which includes teacher leaders, principals, and central office administrators—we must ensure that the instruction occurring in the classroom on a daily basis is equitable and culturally appropriate for all learners.

To make this shift, we must distinguish evaluation (summative) from supervision (formative) and spend more time and resources on the later. Evaluation certainly helps with human resource planning, but it does nothing to actively develop human resources in real time. That is where culturally responsive instructional supervision can be applied, practiced, and implemented to support daily reflection about instructional practices.

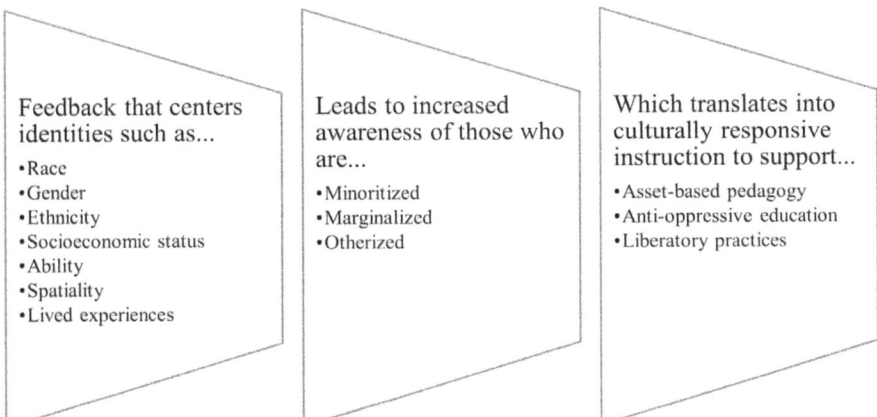

Figure 2.2. Feedback through Instructional Supervision That Leads to Equitable Outcomes

But it does not mean that those with formal positions of power are solely responsible for this shift in thinking about instruction. Rather, instructional leaders who are able to empower others through culturally responsive instructional supervision engage in the difficult work of helping educators make a shift toward understanding and implementing asset-based pedagogies.

UTILIZING ONGOING CONVERSATIONS TO COCREATE KNOWLEDGE AND PROMOTE AUTHENTIC ACCOUNTABILITY

If instructional leaders are to make a shift toward providing culturally responsive instructional supervision, it will require those who provide instruction to children to interrogate and understand their cultural competence and engage in critical self-reflection on how they contribute to and perpetuate hegemonic structures and processes in US society. This will require instructional supervisors to break away from seeing themselves as people in positions of power and instead use human-centered and constructive approaches that allow for facilitating ongoing conversations with teachers about how and in what ways instruction can be seen as a vehicle for liberation and inclusion.

The work of providing feedback about instruction must shift from leveraging power over teachers and instead become providing power to teachers to reflect on their instruction. It also requires discussions about instruction to center on how teaching in the United States can center various forms of identity, such as race, gender, ethnicity, SES, ability, spatiality, and lived experiences of both teachers and students. Ultimately, the cocreation of knowledge about what is considered culturally responsive instruction is an interactive exchange that requires daily reflections on how to empower students who are minoritized to see themselves in the daily lessons provided by teachers.

To disrupt the opportunity gaps that prevent social justice from being achieved in the United States, educators must work together to ensure resources and opportunities are more equitably provided to all students. And to achieve this lofty goal, ongoing professional and personal development through culturally responsive instructional supervision will need to focus on providing safe and vulnerable spaces for educators to reflect on a variety of factors, including but not limited to their own identity, their awareness of inequity in the United States, and how they apply asset-based pedagogies to educate children who come from historically marginalized backgrounds.

LEVERAGING RELATIONAL TRUST TO
PROMOTE MORE INCLUSIVE INSTRUCTION

Throughout this book you will read how to develop and implement a culturally responsive instructional supervision framework in your building. In the upcoming chapters we share our insights on how, as a US education system, we must move away from templates and continuums to drive our improvement efforts and how this can translate into a community of reflective instructors. We will also share why it is important to develop a team of inclusive instructional leaders who are able to provide culturally responsive instructional supervision.

This framework requires schools to move away from the idea that feedback should be provided solely by the principal. Instead, feedback should be provided through the intentional creation of a representative instructional supervision team. It also requires the team to determine the individualized needs of a school based on the students and families the system serves. It also requires establishing a plan of action, intervention, and support when instruction is observed that is not inclusive.

For schools to make this shift, culturally and pedagogically, will require educators to work together in trusting relationships. This means educational leaders—mostly principals but also teacher leaders—must avoid feedback that messages a teacher is "getting in trouble" when they display instruction that lacks cultural responsiveness. To be clear, this does not mean instructors have endless opportunities to improve their instruction if they fail to close the sociocultural gap, but it does mean that feedback needs to be supportive, targeted, and developmentally appropriate.

Throughout the latter part of this book, you will read more about this framework. It includes empowering teachers to target growth that originates from the self, as well as learning how to grow with feedback from critical colleagues. It also values developing a system that honors the vulnerable feedback that can be received from peer-led classroom observations that provide reflections outside of feedback that is provided by the instructional supervision team and the principal.

The goal of culturally responsive instructional supervision, in the long term, is to create a school culture that is naturally inquisitive and signals a school climate that sees instructional improvement as a collective process, one where deprivatization of classroom instruction is not only welcomed but also celebrated. As guardians of inclusion, instructional leaders need to focus on the deregulation of administrative power so that all educators—paraprofessionals, teachers, and building leaders—engage in liberatory education.

There will be, without question, bumps in the road as schoolhouses pivot away from the history of industrialization and toward an organic system that values constructive and supportive feedback about instruction to address the sociocultural gaps in the United States. Teachers will make mistakes, as will principals. However, the point of culturally responsive instructional supervision is not to point out these mistakes, but rather to provide a supportive team structure that allows educators to learn how to "get into good trouble," and that can only occur when trusting relationships promote the development of more inclusive instruction.

In chapter 3, we further the discussion of how the cocreation of knowledge occurs when we move past templates and continuums that are perpetuated through teacher evaluation systems like Marzano and Danielson. Given the racialized and oppressive history of the United States and how that translates into our modern society, feedback about instruction should avoid formulaic metrics and instead focus on developing common language and assumptions about what culturally responsive instruction looks like in classrooms.

Through this work, instructional supervisors can work together with teachers to develop policies, practices, and feedback loops that align with equitable outcomes and redistribute resources to help teachers and students liberate themselves from the high-stakes accountability experiment the United States has engaged in for over two decades.

NOTES

1. Mette, I. M., Aguilar, I., & Wieczorek, D. (2020). A thirty state analysis of teacher supervision and evaluation systems in the ESSA era. *Journal of Educational Supervision, 3*(2), 105–135.

2. Grissom, J. A., & Bartanen, B. (2018). Strategic retention: Principal effectiveness and teacher turnover in multiple-measure teacher evaluation systems. *American Educational Research Journal*, 1–42. https://doi.org/10.3102/0002831218797931

3. Mette, I. M., Range, B. G., Anderson, J., Hvidston, D. J., Nieuwenhuizen, L, & Doty, J. (2017). The wicked problem of the intersection between supervision and evaluation. *International Electronic Journal of Elementary Education, 9*(3), 709–724.

4. Hazi, H. M. (2019). Coming to understand the wicked problem of teacher evaluation. In S. J. Zepeda & J. A. Ponticell (Eds.), *The Wiley handbook of educational supervision* (pp. 183–208). Wiley Blackwell.

5. Milner, IV, H. R. (2008). Critical race theory and interest convergence as analytic tools in teacher education policies and practices. *Journal of Teacher Education, 59*(4), 332–46; and Ladson–Billings, G. (1999). Preparing teachers for diverse student populations: A critical race theory perspective. *Review of Research in Education, 24*, 211–247.

6. Khalifa, M. (2020). *Culturally responsive school leadership* (4th ed.). Harvard Education Press; and Ladson–Billings, G. (1998). Just what is critical race theory and what's it doing in a nice field like education? *Qualitative Studies in Education,* *11*(1), 7–24.

7. Schwartz, S. (2021). 8 states debate bills to restrict how teachers discuss racism, sexism. *Education Week.* https://www.edweek.org/policy-politics/8-states-debate-bills-to-restrict-how-teachers-discuss-racism-sexism/2021/04

8. Khalifa, M. (2020). *Culturally responsive school leadership* (4th ed.). Harvard Education Press.

9. Freire, P. (1970). *Pedagogy of the oppressed.* Seabury Press.

Chapter 3

Liberating Ourselves from Prepackaged Systems

One of the most damning aspects of providing feedback about instruction since the inception of NCLB is the embedded belief that education should function more like a business and that business structures and practices will improve student outcomes in the United States. These ideologies are incredibly destructive on multiple levels. Over the course of the accountability experiment that was formalized and enacted starting in 2001, education has witnessed a dramatic increase in the use of prepackaged curricula aligned directly with high-stakes tests.

The accountability experiment has allowed for a corporate model for accountability to infiltrate the US education system, providing entry points that allow businesses to control what is taught, how it is taught, and how it is measured. Education has undergone a significant transformation through corporate interest and subsequent influence via economic and political levers. As a result, financial considerations and philosophical foundations have come to play a significant role in determining curriculum and instructional practices.

Not only have the interests of corporate entities benefited through the selling of prepacked curricula about *what* teachers teach and *how* students learn, corporate profits have also driven how teachers are evaluated and provided feedback about their instruction. Ask any teacher who has experienced evaluation, or any principal who has provided teacher evaluation, about the practices of prepacked teacher evaluation systems since the implementation of ESSA and you will hear a wide variety of criticism.

Most notably you will hear complaints about the use of templates and continuums. These prescribed protocols attempt to place teacher performance on a standardized curve, suggesting that few teachers can (or *should*) ever reach the top level of a ranking scale. Additionally, these templates and continuums focus overwhelmingly on prescribed domains and standardization, suggesting there is one way (and one way only) to teach students well. What the major prepacked teacher evaluation systems do not provide insight about, notably Marzano and Danielson, but certainly including others, is to how to teach students in a way that is culturally responsive and appropriate.

WHY MOVING BEYOND THE
CHECKLIST IS SO IMPORTANT

To help provide instructional supervision that allows educators to think critically about closing the sociocultural gap and subsequent opportunity gaps, instructional leaders need to first free themselves from the beliefs and values of prepackaged teacher evaluation systems that lack any inclusion of how to support instruction that is inclusive, culturally responsive, and leads to more equitable outcomes for the diverse group of students served in the US public education system. When considering how to provide ongoing, formative feedback about improving instruction, educators must go beyond thinking about learning objectives, structures, routines, and evidence of learning.

While traditional aims of formative feedback are certainly important and have their place in considering how teachers can consider how students learn, instructional supervisors must move beyond relying on checklists and engage in the daily or weekly work of providing feedback about what is observed in the classroom as it relates to supporting teachers to critically reflect on what is taught and how it is relevant to students who live in the community the school serves.[1]

To help teachers make sense of pedagogical practices, culturally responsive instructional supervision needs to consider race, gender, ethnicity, SES, ability, spatiality, and the lived experiences of students, specifically how teachers can learn to develop "knowledge, attitudes, dispositions, beliefs, skills, and practices necessary to meet student needs."[2] Given that two of the most popular teacher evaluation models in the United States were written by White educators, it should perhaps not be surprising that these prescribed continuums and checklists lack inclusion and centering of minoritized, marginalized, and otherized students' sociocultural beliefs and identities.

Supposed "race-neutral" approaches to improving teaching prevent teachers and administrators from understanding the individual needs of the community they serve,[3] and in fact contribute to the idea that traditional education systems serve to control historically marginalized groups. Figure 3.1 highlights how culturally responsive instructional supervision can center the voice of the marginalized, encourage educators to self-reflect on privileged identities, and acknowledge students show comprehension in ways that are not prescribed or standardized. As such, moving beyond a prescribed checklist

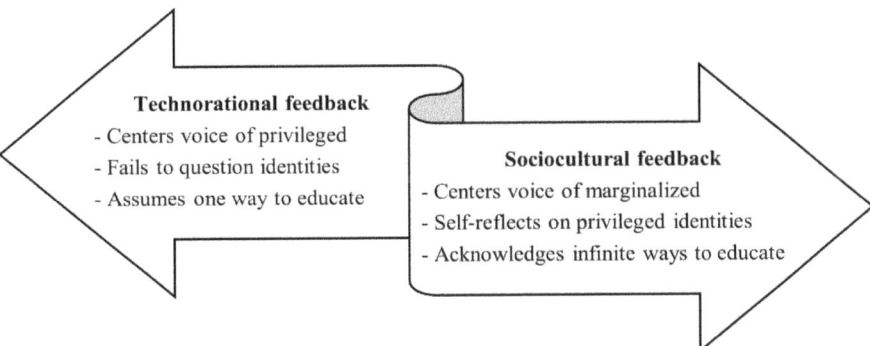

Figure 3.1.   Traditional Evaluation vs. Culturally Responsive Instructional Supervision

about what is considered "good" instruction is central to the instructional leadership needed to provide culturally responsive instructional supervision.

To make the shift away from technorational instructional improvement efforts, instructional leaders should closely examine and critique the framework of feedback used in their school or school system. Does the feedback framework center the voices of the privileged, or does it seek to uplift the voice of the historically marginalized? Does it ignore how identity impacts the way feedback is provided and perceived or does it encourage those providing feedback to question their privileged identities? Does it assume or explicitly state there is one way to be a "good" educator, or does it acknowledge there are infinite ways to provide liberatory, asset-based, and antioppressive education? These critical questions must be asked if instructional leaders want to support more inclusive instruction in the schoolhouse.

HOW TEMPLATES PREVENT CRITICAL THINKING

Given there is no major prepackaged teacher evaluation system currently that asks teachers to reflect on how their sociocultural identities influence the way they think about instruction, it is all the more important for instructional leaders to engage in reflective practices that help educators engage in critical thinking and self-reflection in this important work.[4] When educators fail to use reflective practices to question how power and privilege influence their teaching, dominant identities (whiteness, class, ability, etc.) are continually recentered through a wide variety of policies and practices.[5]

As such, the use of templates to drive conceptualization and paradigms about what are considered good instructional practices completely ignores the lived realities of students who are minoritized, marginalized, and otherized. What results is the continuation of oppressive instructional practices that fail to acknowledge the role instruction plays in developing antioppressive school systems.

However, to implement culturally responsive instructional supervision, instructional leaders must move away from feedback templates that fail to center the voices of the minoritized, marginalized, and otherized. If you were to examine prepackaged teacher feedback systems, such as Marzano and Danielson, and conducted a keyword search for diversity, equity, inclusion, race, and identity (just to name a few), you would find little to no evidence that either of these mainstream feedback systems even mentions these words.

Further complicating the matter, feedback about instruction from students, parents, peer teachers, or administrators can never be static because the needs of the students and families are dynamic and circumstantial. Consequently, schools' responses to students' and families' needs constantly change and evolve. Instead, teachers and instructional supervisors need to engage in ongoing dialogue about instructional practices that increase inclusiveness and humanize students[6] and cannot be beholden to a template that says there are set ways to adhere to rules, procedures, "management" of student behavior, arrangement of the physical class environment, or assessment of student knowledge.

LEARNING TO CREATE FEEDBACK PRACTICES THAT ARE IMMEDIATELY USEFUL

You might be getting to the point where you are asking yourself, "So if templates and continuums prevent critical feedback, how are teachers supposed to receive feedback about their instruction so they can implement new practices the next day?" Part of the answer to this question goes back to what we shared in chapter 2, where feedback must shift from a traditional model of being seen as hierarchical and move toward an ecological model that values feedback from all points of the environment.

If we constantly receive feedback about top-down, policy-driven instruction that is reminiscent of a business production model, we will only reinforce ideologies that center privileged groups or structures. Figure 3.2 underscores how culturally responsive instructional supervisors can create a culture of self-reflection that values ongoing discussions about instruction based on observable data collection, and that through structured self-reflection can lead to changes in teaching practices and implementation of more humanizing instruction. What we must seek instead is feedback through instructional supervision that actively searches to center the voice of those who are minoritized, marginalized, and otherized.

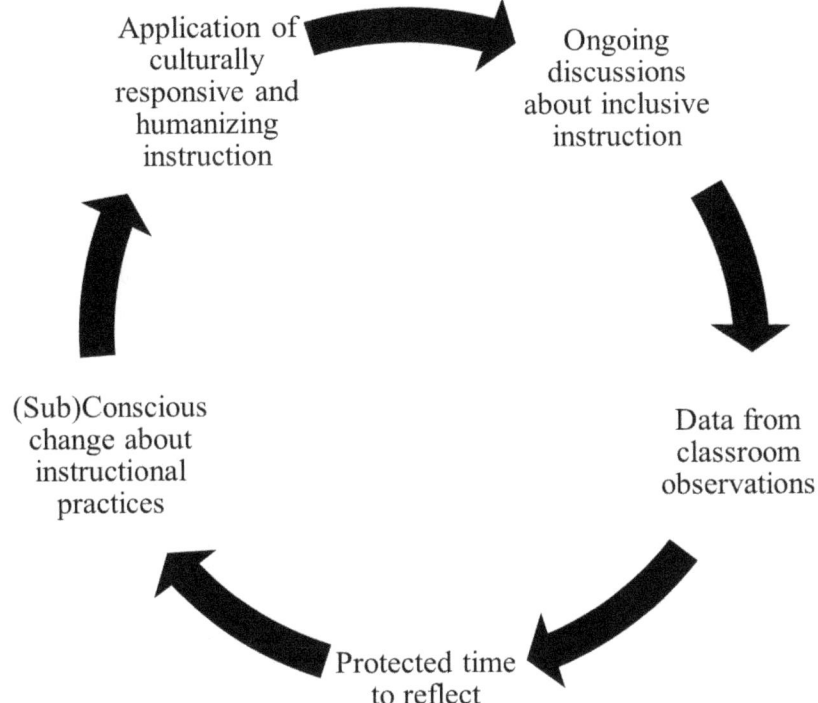

Figure 3.2. Culturally Responsive Instructional Supervision Self-Study Cycle

While we will expand more on the formal development of an intentionally representative supervision team in chapter 5, as well as how to measure and assess quantitative and qualitative data to ensure more equitable outcomes occur in chapter 6, instructional supervisors can help teachers reflect on their instructional practices through practical, everyday data points. These include increasing student voice, assessing authentic community engagement, as well as how peer-to-peer feedback about instructional practices can ensure that students see themselves in the curriculum and that an inclusive instructional environment is created, maintained, and protected.

We want to highlight the focus on the connection to the human element here. If education is to ever play a role in making US society more equitable, it must come through ongoing discussions, collecting data points during classroom observations and allowing teachers to analyze the data themselves, and providing protected moments of reflection that allow educators to disrupt their own (sub)conscious contribution to hidden curriculum that perpetuates sociocultural and opportunity gaps, which actively prevents educators from increasing their cultural competence.[7]

Presented above is a self-study cycle that empowers and enables an educator to actively engage in critical self-reflection about how their teaching is influenced by their own privileges afforded to them by their identities. To accomplish this goal, instructional supervisors must consider how adult learners learn to change their behavior best. Mezirow[8] posits that adults who participate in critical self-reflection can engage in transformational learning that results in changed beliefs and practices—in this case culturally responsive instruction.

However, without ongoing feedback about instruction that values vulnerability and celebrates learning about sociocultural factors in real time, it is highly unlikely that teachers will instinctively alter how they think about and provide instruction. Culturally responsive instructional supervision must be something instructional leaders engage in repeatedly, and the first step in this process is to develop explicit assumptions about culturally responsive instruction that can drive dialogue and the exchange of ideas.

DEVELOPING COMMON LANGUAGE AND ASSUMPTIONS ABOUT LEARNING

To liberate ourselves from continuums and templates, and to break the cycle of reinforcement that suggests there is one way to teach effectively, we must develop a language to have these discussions. This means that we need to question how often we assess children and how we create student engagement about social injustices and inequities that exist in our local communities, our state, our country, and the world more broadly. It also means we need to seriously question how to shape, manipulate, and control students' behavior, especially when students disengage with learning because they do not see themselves in the curriculum.

In developing a language for how we talk about learning, we must be able to engage in critical conversations and discussions about race, gender, ethnicity, SES, ability, spatiality, and lived experiences, among other aspects of identity. While these conversations can be uncomfortable and will surely create difficult reflections about instructional practices in real time, these reflections are the foundation for educators to discuss how they might work together to close the sociocultural gap in the United States. Questions that educators should be willing to ask each other about instructional practices include but are not limited to

- Are we aware of our privileged identities as educators, and do we consider them as we develop our lesson plans?

- How will our students who are minoritized, marginalized, and otherized interpret our lesson plans, and will these students see themselves in curricula products and subsequent instruction?
- How are we as educators considering the role of race in our lesson plans, and do we make explicit space to discuss the role of race in the United States through our lessons?
- How do we engage in questions about male dominance, and how do we make space for female voices, as well as lesbian, gay, bisexual, transgender, queer, intersex, and allied/asexual/aromantic/agender (LGBTQIA+) voices in our lessons?
- How do we consider how racial and ethnic identities influence cultural traditions, especially in the United States, where European Christian values are dominant?
- How do our lesson plans and expectations about learning outside of the schoolhouse account for SES?
- As educators, are we aware of ableist expectations or language that can be discriminatory and exclusionary?
- Do we consider how spatiality, specifically the interaction between the lived environment and available resources, influences asset-based learning that can be tailored to leverage students' strengths and cultural assets?

To fully address the questions listed above and develop a common language to implement culturally responsive instructional supervision, instructional leaders must work together and collaborate about the exchange of ideas and language used to unpack these ideas. This requires educators to actively value and seek out a diverse range of coworkers who can acknowledge how their own experiences, identities, lenses, roles, and lived experiences in different regions of the United States influence their approaches to education and instruction more specifically.

Once educators begin these discussions, committed educators can begin the ongoing task of addressing the social, racial, and economic inequities that exist throughout the US education system. It is only through the intentional development of a common language that questions and challenges assumptions about education that teachers and administrators can change policies and practices that are discriminatory in nature. And while there are policy requirements we must legally address as public education systems, we can do so in a way that supports pedagogy and produces more equitable outcomes.

MEETING POLICY REQUIREMENTS THROUGH
PEDAGOGIES THAT LEAD TO EQUITABLE OUTCOMES

To help move US society forward, schools must transition to being places of healing, growth, and sustenance.[9] If true democracy is to be attained, one that honors the voices and histories of all its people, including Asian, Black, Indigenous, Latinx, and White citizens, school leaders in the United States will need to free themselves from paradigms of educational leadership that perpetuates education as a system of oppression.

One of the most direct ways instructional leaders can drive these changes is by leveraging the existing laws and policies of the education system itself. As noted earlier, all states have teacher supervision and evaluation systems that require oversight of instruction that are intended to improve the instruction of teachers.[10] Through these intentions, instructional leaders can make a conscious decision to meet technical requirements of policies but in a way that promotes pedagogies that can be used in meaningful ways to acknowledge and address the historical societal structures that have perpetuated inequities in the United States.

School districts can help by shifting the work of instructional coaches away from simply focusing on math and reading. Using an equity-minded approach, school systems can redistribute a portion of these resources to ensure equitable and inclusive instruction is also occurring in social studies, science, and elective classes. Additionally, central office personnel can target creating a school budget that provides additional professional development to teacher leaders and principals to increase training on sociocultural competence.

Central to this idea is the shift away from ahistorical education that is considered "clinical." Instead, feedback about instruction should focus on the support of rigorous instruction and exploration for students to develop a deeper understanding of their own identities. Additionally, professional development should actively engage teachers to provide instruction that addresses issues of social justice throughout our society.[11]

As a result, there is an opportunity for instructional supervision practices to become historical and political, and to support a community of reflective instructors who can engage in their own sociocultural development to mitigate ongoing bias and sociocultural gaps. Instructional supervisors can support teachers in expanding their reflective stances about their instruction, specifically how it relates to respective identities, cultures, and societal expectations throughout the United States. In chapter 4, we discuss the importance of creating a community of reflective instructors, one that sees learning together as a form of love but also serves as a reminder of the need to liberate our society now.

NOTES

1. Ladson–Billings, G. (1998). Just what is critical race theory and what's it doing in a nice field like education? *Qualitative Studies in Education, 11*(1), 7–24; Ladson-Billings, G. (2017). The (r)evolution will not be standardized. In D. Paris & H. S. Alim (Eds.), *Culturally sustaining pedagogies: Teaching and learning for justice in a changing world* (pp. 141–56). Teachers College Press.

2. Milner, IV, H. R. (2017). Where's the race in culturally relevant pedagogy? *Teachers College Record, 119*, 1–32.

3. Watson, T. N., & Nash, A. M. (2021). Challenging whiteness at Claremont High School. *Journal of Cases in Educational Leadership, 24*(3), 3–14.

4. Khalifa, M. (2020). *Culturally responsive school leadership* (4th ed.). Harvard Education Press.

5. Gooden, M. A., & Dantley, M. (2012). Centering race in a framework for leadership preparation. *Journal of Research on Leadership Education, 7*(2), 237–53.

6. Khalifa, M. (2020). *Culturally responsive school leadership* (4th ed.). Harvard Education Press.

7. Cormier, D. R. (2022). Prototyping the Cultural Proficiency Continuum Dialogic Protocol with professional development school teacher interns. *Urban Education.* https://doi.org/10.1177/00420859221140405; Jay, M. (2003). Critical race theory, multicultural education, and the hidden curriculum of hegemony. *Multicultural Perspectives, 5*(4), 3–9.

8. Mezirow, J. (2009). Transformative learning theory. In J. Mezirow & E. W. Taylor (Eds.), *Transformative learning in practice: Insights from community, workplace, and higher education* (pp. 18–32). Jossey-Bass.

9. Alim, H. S., & Paris, D. (2017). What is culturally sustaining pedagogy and why does it matter? In D. Paris & H. S. Alim (Eds.), *Teaching and learning for justice in a changing world* (pp. 1–24). Teachers College Press.

10. Mette, I. M., Aguilar, I., & Wieczorek, D. (2020). A thirty state analysis of teacher supervision and evaluation systems in the ESSA era. *Journal of Educational Supervision, 3*(2), 105–35.

11. Alim, H. S., & Paris, D. (2017). What is culturally sustaining pedagogy and why does it matter? In D. Paris & H. S. Alim (Eds.), *Teaching and learning for justice in a changing world* (pp. 1–24). Teachers College Press.

Chapter 4

Learning to Engage in a Community of Culturally Responsive Instructors

The idea of moving past externally imposed forms of high-stakes accountability efforts, specifically from state or federal authorities, is crucial to developing a community of educators who are constantly willing to reflect on their own instructional practices. Leadership from teacher leaders, principals, and central office administrators is needed to help make this shift in culture and in practice. And at the heart of this paradigm shift are the structures and supports that can be implemented to ensure teachers are accountable to reflect on their own instructional practices to help make student learning more equitable, engaging, and empowering.

To create a community of culturally responsive instructors (CCRIs), educators need to develop introspective practices that allow them to deeply critique their practices and how these practices are perceived by students. Educators need to be aware of and collect their own instructional data—and not wait to be given observation data by another educator in a position of power—that can help them further their reflective stance development. Examples include assigning readings of authors who come from historically marginalized groups, reviewing historical accounts from Black, Indigenous, and Latinx perspectives, and studying math problems that highlight inequities.

Of course, high-quality instruction goes beyond simple equity counts. To be more equitable and inclusive of all students, a shift that must happen in US schools among educators is to make their classrooms more open, inviting, and engaging—for both students and peers to observe. While quantitative data can lead to great improvement efforts to better instruction, qualitative data can also provide great data for a community of reflective educators. For example, using qualitative data to examine how teachers discuss issues of

inequity with students or use students' cultural knowledge to enhance curricula products and subsequent instruction and student learning.

So what can be done to help the US education system shift away from
hierarchical feedback systems and toward feedback loops that are constructive and seen as helpful? And what does it mean for educators to liberate
themselves from templates and continuums, and instead engage with each
other as a CCRI? At the core of this work, it requires instructional leadership
that is willing to *empower* teachers to collect and reflect on data they gather
and analyze themselves, and in doing so support educational practices that
consider a more equitable society and resist dogmatic practices that reinforce
destructive narratives about cultural identities.

CONSIDERING THE ROLE OF DATA IN
ACTS OF EDUCATIONAL RESISTANCE

Data, specifically quantitative data, has been seen historically as a tool to
"level the playing field" of education. Many early proponents of data-driven
education believed that with enough time, instructional gaps between
demographic groups—by race, SES, and those receiving special education
services—would be closed over time.[1] In practice, this has not happened.
Instead, education has experienced an incredible uptick in deficit mindsets
and pedagogical practices that benefit those with privileged sociocultural
identities because of prescribed data collection, particularly around testing,
the use of grades, and access to advanced coursework.

To create a CCRI—a context that encourages self-reflection and learning
from one another as professionals—educators must shift their paradigms
about what is measured, quantified, analyzed, and reflected upon (in addition
to considering collecting and analyzing qualitative data largely missing from
PK–12 settings). This means measuring things we know matter in public
schools, using an assets-based approach to instruction, and then acting on the
data meaningfully to make instruction more equitable and accessible. Making
this shift can be seen as acts of resistance to oppressive education systems,
to include when

- Curricular inputs and outcomes are deeply questioned, specifically
  asking if there is student representation and inclusion beyond White,
  Eurocentric perspectives;
- Access to advanced coursework is prioritized for students who are
  minoritized, marginalized, and otherized, and adjustments are made to
  support students who remain enrolled in these courses;

- Culturally responsive practices are measured through walkthroughs and tracked through data analysis as a form of accountability;
- Student and parent perceptions are welcomed as a form of feedback through survey data, and student and parent cultural assets and differences are leveraged within the community a school serves; and
- Extracurricular activities are considered part of the whole school experience, and students who are minoritized, marginalized, and otherized are ensured equal representation and barriers to access (e.g., transportation, necessary equipment) are removed.

To engage in this work, educators in a school community must ask and answer the important questions: "What is taught, how is it taught, and who benefits from what is being taught?" Questioning the role of data and *how the data is used* is critical to creating a CCRI. And moving away from prescribed data collection to a framework that celebrates questions of equity and decentering privileged identities is of utmost importance.[2]

WHY AUTONOMY IS AT THE HEART OF INCLUSIVE INSTRUCTION

For schools that are ready to engage in culturally responsive instructional supervision, there is foundational work to be engaged in, particularly around the autonomy that must be created, fostered, and developed by instructional leaders. Any educator who has taught from 2001 forward has been imprinted with the idea that there is accountability data that should be collected to drive school decisions and improvement practices and that little other data collection matters. Not only are these paradigms harmful to equitable outcomes for students, but they also reinforce groupthink and prevent creativity to solve issues of instructional engagement.

By encouraging teachers to collect and reflect on their own data, collected by peers and self-collected, schools that are engaged in culturally responsive teaching are creating infinite action research projects that will lead to more equitable outcomes *based on the needs of individualized communities*. While it is important to engage with peers in reflecting about culturally responsive instructional practices, every educator must also take responsibility for this learning at the personal level.[3] As such, personalized learning, based on values and beliefs, must first be explored, studied, and refined before learning can occur and ideas can be exchanged in larger groups.

Although it might seem counterintuitive to allow teachers the autonomy to collect their own data to develop more inclusive instructional practices across an entire school, it is important to allow a cross-pollination of ideas to circulate, continuously, throughout a school building. The job of instructional leaders then becomes providing support and development of this type of climate and culture, one where ideas are continuously circulated and practices evolve and adapt over time. And it is through the sharing of ideas, reinforced and confirmed through reflection of various points of data, that a school system can move from accountability to responsibility.

By celebrating and supporting the autonomy of teachers, instructional leaders can develop a team of educators who are dedicated to continually improving their practice. As a group of professionals, teachers are responsible for continually questioning their own practices by being appropriately self-critical and by acknowledging how their privileged identities influence their approach to teaching and the outcomes they hope to accomplish through their classroom instruction. Once teachers start this work on their own, they can then begin the important process of developing a CCRI by sharing their approaches in small groups.

HOW CRITICAL COLLEAGUES CAN COLLABORATE FOR CO-LIBERATION

While great learning can occur from teacher to teacher, the reflections gained from analyzing data at the individualized classroom level will remain isolated and in silos unless educators are able to share the lessons learned of their self-collected data and reflections. However, if structured correctly by instructional leaders in a building, reflection at the individual level can help create entry points for other like-minded individuals to glom onto each other and form a larger group of educators who are willing to engage in critical work as a small team. Together, these critical colleagues can engage in reflective practices that add the CCRI within the school culture and building.

A team of critical colleagues should be developed based on interest in specific equity goals or outputs, approaches to data collection, and instructional practices specific to reflective stances to improve instruction. Unlike a traditional professional learning community (PLC), critical colleagues do not need to be aligned based on content area or grade level. In fact, there will be more authentic connection and work accomplished in the name of equity if the critical colleague collaboration team forms because it wants to learn from each other[4]—not because it is forced to by formal leadership.

It is in these smaller groups of educators—somewhere between three to five teachers, teacher leaders, and/or administrators—that deeper learning can occur about liberatory practices that can happen within the classroom. Figure 4.1 details the power of teacher autonomy to drive learning both individually and with critical colleague groups to develop more liberatory practices in the

Figure 4.1.   **Teacher Autonomy as a Foundation for Critical Colleague Collaborations**

schoolhouse. By this we mean two things, namely, liberation from the failed accountability experiment that has occurred since 2001 and liberation from an education system that has systematically minoritized, marginalized, and otherized students in the United States.[5] The work that could occur in these critical colleague collaborations might include:

- Reteaching a mathematics concept across subject areas using an integrated approach to underscore historic differences of access to resources among racial groups and then discussing the root causes in a manner than empowers students to enact change;
- Analyzing discipline data by teachers and working together with administrators to address spikes in observed behavior that can be solved through parent meetings to share what is occurring and form more of a community-based approach to support student needs;
- Collaborating in vertical content teams to discuss skills learned the previous year, key objectives that should be met in the current year, and what will need to be learned in the upcoming year to ensure student success is maximized;
- Discussing the gap that occurs in extracurricular activities, particularly among racial and SES lines, and how community groups might work more collaboratively with teachers and parents to eliminate a lack of access and/or maximize participation.

Through the work that critical colleagues engage in, pockets of reflective practitioners emerge and create *their own feedback loops about instruction.*

These groups are then able to sustain questions of equity and wrestle with answers to more inclusive instruction that simply cannot be provided through the current high-stakes accountability approach to education. And it is through this kind of work—where pockets of equity are allowed to emerge organically—that a school culture can be shifted over time to ensure that all students have access to a more inclusive and representative educational experience.

SHARING LEARNING AS A FORM OF
LOVE ACROSS A SCHOOL CULTURE

Supporting the development of a CCRI requires instructional leaders who can encourage introspection at the individual level, within critical colleague collaborations, and perhaps most important, can bring groups of educators together and engage in the process of developing a more clearly defined school culture that yields culturally responsive and appropriate outcomes. Learning does not stop at the individual level or among critical colleagues, but rather there is an opportunity to create synergy among the pockets of reflection and create a larger learning exchange. As such, instructional leaders have an opportunity to magnify the reflective practices that emerge organically within pockets across a school culture.

To accomplish this lofty goal, educators in general, but more specifically principals, will need to continue to flatten the hierarchy of the education system and allow for greater leadership to emerge from within the ranks of teachers. Top-down professional development rarely is successfully implemented beyond a one to two year period and often is resisted by faculty who believe "this too shall pass." Creating a CCRI requires not only principals to trust teacher leaders to enact change and empower them with autonomy and agency but also instructional leaders to create a culture that sees sharing about learning and instruction as a *form of love*.[6]

At this point you might be asking yourself, what exactly does love have to do with creating a CCRI and a school culture that is driven by reflective practices? In short, the answer is everything. Since the early 2000s, schools have continually become places that are hyperfocused on producing achievement outcomes while simultaneously being told by state and federal accountability measures that they should be places that are apolitical and ahistorical. Nothing could be farther from the truth, and to create equitable outcomes for all students, education systems need to support multifaceted investigations to unlearn the deficit-minded accountability paradigm.[7]

If schools in the United States are ever to become part of the solution to addressing the historical inequities that underpin our society, and if they are to move away from prescribed measures of control that have done nothing to close the gap in educational outcomes between various demographic groups within the country, we must stop pretending that there is one "answer" to education. Given this reality, teachers should not need to convince administrators they have potential solutions to addressing inequities in their schools, but rather administrators should encourage teachers to engage in acts of love to address these inequities.

So what do acts of love look like, specifically as it relates to learning across a school culture? A few examples are provided below as suggestions for instructional leaders to consider as they implement culturally responsive instructional supervision and feedback about pedagogy:

- Engaging in deep conversations about grading practices across departments and teams to ensure grades are tied to achievement (scores based on clearly defined rubrics and creative application of objectives) and not tied to effort (points being taken off for needing to charge laptop in class, reduction in classroom participation points for not engaging in classroom discussion, etc.);
- Developing schoolwide practices that create schedules of student assessment to prevent periods of overwhelming and unreasonable study habits of students, as well as create discussion about what is done with the data collected, particularly the remediation provided by teachers based on mastery of objectives or lack thereof;
- Creating meaningful opportunities for parental engagement within the schoolhouse, particularly for parents who come from historically marginalized groups or who can only attend school-based functions outside of the typical workday (often, these are best coordinated and developed with community-based groups);
- Implementing alternative methods of instruction that maximize engagement and minimize disruptive behaviors, particularly for students who benefit from online learning that reduces social anxiety, maximizes opportunities for student success, and maintains after-school extracurricular participation.

None of these alternative ways of thinking can happen, however, unless instructional leaders are willing to allow educators to engage in acts of love, at the individual level, in small groups, and across a school building to find greater equity in the work that can be accomplished in the schoolhouse and for *all children* to see themselves in the curriculum and the instruction[8] that is provided from one classroom to another.

The autonomy that is needed to break away from the traditions of high-stakes accountability is crucial for instructional leaders and that can only come from supporting educators to think critically about educational outcomes and with love for children. In order for school systems to move forward with inclusive instruction, systemic inequities must be questioned from multiple perspectives and vantage points.

QUESTIONING POWER STRUCTURES TO ADDRESS SYSTEMIC INEQUITY

Through the development of a CCRI, teachers, teacher leaders, principals, and central office personnel can develop a multifaceted group of educators who are willing to, through ongoing exploration, question, problematize, experiment, and ultimately begin to deconstruct the systems of inequity that have always existed in US education but that have been exasperated since the inception of NCLB. We know that to meet the needs of students, we must diversify our perspectives and the voices of those engaged in the work of making schools more equitable for students. And that can only come from a CCRI that encourages all educators to question equity.

As mentioned previously, most schools are incredibly hierarchical and put the onus of providing feedback about instruction on the principal. Not only does this reinforce the privilege and power of formal leadership, leading to teachers feeling disenfranchised and devalued for not having their professional opinions considered, but it also recenters privileged sociocultural identities as 80 percent of principals are in the United States are White.[9] Given these realities, it is critical that school systems allow multiple educators from a wide variety of vantage points to question inequitable practices and collaborate on openly resisting inequitable practices.

When instructional leaders empower teachers to question how the reflection of their instructional practices might lead to more equitable and culturally responsive outcomes, as well as give them the autonomy to collect data about their own instructional practices, they are creating a core foundation that addresses the feedback loop problem in US schools. Rather than waiting for a principal to provide feedback about their instruction, instructional leaders can give power to teachers rather than maintain power over them. In doing so, instructional leaders can empower individuals to drive their own reflection, encourage translation of these practices to other teachers, and impact a school culture on a much broader level (see figure 4.2).

To accomplish this paradigm shift in leadership, principals need to move away from managerial approaches and readily acknowledge the massively important role they can play in helping create more inclusive instruction in

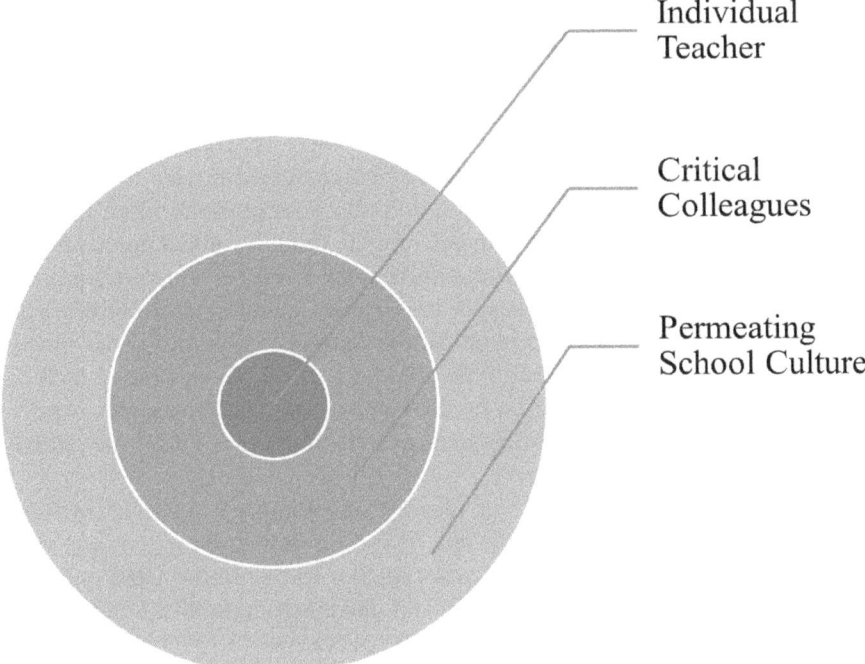

Individual
Teacher

Critical
Colleagues

Permeating
School Culture

Figure 4.2.   Multifaceted Approach to Developing a Culture of Reflection

their building. This is not as hard as some people might make it out to be—a successful principal does not need to be an expert in math or language arts to be a good instructional leader. However, they do need to engage in *creating structures* that will help empower teachers gaining and applying expertise through culturally responsive instructional supervision in order for every student in their building to be successful.[10]

By flattening the hierarchy of schools, instructional leaders—both formal and informal—can provide critique of inequitable instructional practices and policies in real time. Not only will this help to maximize inclusion and belonging in schools, but it creates an organic structure for educators at all levels to be critical of their own practices, as well as provide a safe space to help other educators through the development of a CCRI. In many ways this work goes beyond the siloed approaches of traditional PLCs and breaks down learning barriers between grade levels, content areas, and ideological groups that often occurs within schoolhouses.

THE CHALLENGES OF MOVING
FORWARD WITH THE WORK

The previous three chapters address the feedback loop problems that are systemic in schools throughout the United States. When instructional leaders flatten the hierarchy of schools, they empower educators to reexamine the purpose of feedback about instruction and help promote more inclusive instruction for all students. To foster critical thinking about inclusion and a sense of belonging, we propose a shift away from reliance on templates, continuums, and checklists. Instead, we propose developing a more organic process that challenges assumptions about learning outcomes. This process and approach encourage a more nuanced and holistic perspective, which can better address the complexities of diverse learning environments. And by supporting autonomy to question inclusive instruction, a CCRI can address systemic inequities.

In the following chapters, the idea of developing a team of inclusive instructional leaders will be reviewed, including how to be intentional about representation, how schools can work together to determine what culturally responsive instructional supervision and feedback look like, and how to establish a plan of action when instruction is observed to be culturally damaging or destructive. In these chapters, questions will be proposed that ask educators to answer important questions about instruction, including

- Why does intentional representation matter when giving feedback about instruction?
- What "look fors" should be included when considering culturally responsive instruction?
- How should instructional leaders balance morale while also not centering privileged identities?
- How can data collection about instruction be determined in a truly democratic fashion?
- What methods can be used to empower all teachers to examine instructional data more critically?
- How can instructional leaders support educators in questioning assumptions about what "good teaching" looks like?
- What can be done to position critical self-reflection as a tool for growth rather than a weapon for fear?

To be an instructional leader who puts equity at the forefront of all leadership decisions will require educators to move past the failed accountability experiment. And this will take time, energy, and persistence. But if schools are to promote culturally responsive teaching, instructional leaders must have deep conversations to increase understanding about who public education in the United States does and does not privilege. It is that act of resistance—of learning to stand up to societal inequities and systems of oppression—that is at the heart of implementing culturally responsive instructional supervision.

NOTES

1. Glickman, C. D., & Mette, I. M. (2020). *The essential renewal of America's schools: A leadership guide for democratizing schools from the inside out*. Teachers College Press.

2. Carter Andrews, D. J., He, Y., Marciano, J. E., Richmond, G., & Salazar, M. (2021). Decentering whiteness in teacher education: Addressing the questions of who, with whom, and how. *Journal of Teacher Education, 72*(2), 134–137.

3. Villegas, A. M., & Lucas, T. (2002). Preparing culturally responsive teachers: Rethinking the curriculum. *Journal of Teacher Education, 53*(1), 20–32.

4. Cooper, K. S., Stanulis, R. N., Brondyk, S. K., Hamilton, E. R., Mascaluso, M., & Meier, J. A. (2018). The teacher leadership process: Attempting change within embedded systems. *Journal of Educational Change, 17*, 85–113.

5. Love, B. L. (2019b). *We want to do more than survive: Abolitionist teaching and the pursuit of educational reform*. Beacon Press.

6. Muhammad, G. (2022). On identity. *Voices From the Middle, 30*(1), 14–16.

7. Milner, IV, H. R. (2020). *Start where you are, but don't stay there: Understanding diversity, opportunity gaps, and teaching in today's classrooms* (2nd ed.). Harvard Education Press.

8. Love, B. L. (2019). Dear White teachers: You can't love your Black students if you don't know them. *Education Week, 38*(26), 18.

9. National Center for Education Statistics (NCES). (2016). Characteristics of public school teachers. https://nces.ed.gov/programs/coe/indicator_clr.asp.

10. Radd, S. I., Generett, G. G., Gooden, M. A., & Theoharis, G. (2021). *Five practices for equity-focused school leadership*. ASCD.

PART II

Developing a Team of Inclusive Instructional Leaders

Chapter 5

Being Intentional about Representation

US society has always struggled to openly acknowledge and discuss the gross inequities that permeate our various social systems—including but not limited to the legal, economic, political, healthcare, and education systems. Those with sociocultural identities that these systems protect, namely, those who identify as White, cisgender, heterosexual, male, middle-to-upper class, able-bodied, and of Western European decent, typically struggle to conceptualize how social systems are seen as oppressive. And yet there is plenty of research that underscores how this plays out in the US education system and the impact this has on all students.[1]

Many US citizens believed that after the election and reelection of President Obama, the first Black president in US history, US society had entered a "postracial" society.[2] (Since that time, US politics has engaged in enacting policies that have challenged access to equal voting rights, promoted anti-immigration policies, challenged access to women's rights, and promoted anti-CRT bills that prevent equity-centered discussion about race.[3] These policies challenge educators' ability throughout the United States to implement equity-based instruction that is inclusive for all students—not just those who are privileged.

For the US education system to address the inequities that are present and to address the privileged sociocultural identities that wield enormous power within our society, US educators need to consider how representation matters in terms of how instruction is conceptualized and how feedback about instruction is provided. To be clear, those with privileged identities do not need to be ashamed or embarrassed by their identities—but they do need to acknowledge these identities. To expedite this, instructional leaders must consider how to flatten the hierarchy and *structure* of feedback to make instructional decisions with a representative team.

WHY REPRESENTATION MATTERS

To better understand how to provide equitable and inclusive instruction within the United States, educators need to acknowledge how race, gender, ethnicity, socioeconomic status, ability, and spatiality (among other identities) influence the lived experiences of students, parents, and community members who are minoritized, marginalized, and otherized. By acknowledging how privileged identities influence the conceptualization of how instruction is provided and perceived, educators can and should consider why representation matters when providing feedback about instruction. And to better understand diverse perspectives, representation should be centered and valued.

So why should educators be concerned with representation? And why, specifically, should instructional leaders focus on being intentional about representation when considering how they provide feedback about implementing culturally responsive instructional practices? While these questions center around complex social structures, the fact is we often need the perspectives of others with different lived experiences to consider how equitable and inclusive instruction can lead to a greater sense of belonging, specifically as it relates to the experiences of students, parents, and community members.

Central to this work is the idea of creating a group of trusted colleagues who can create a feedback loop, built off the idea of a CCRI, that supports learning through vulnerability. Instead of instructional feedback that is punitive, one that all too often focuses on an "I got you" approach, culturally responsive instructional supervision should allow all educators to see feedback about culturally responsive instruction as an opportunity for growth and development and not a punishment for a lack of awareness. There is no quick answer for this work, and it requires a lot of time and effort to create a system that allows for critique, and not criticism, about instruction.

To better conceptualize why representation matters for providing culturally responsive instructional supervision, educators can think about feedback based on the idea of a societal mosaic. When feedback is disproportionately provided by any one sociocultural identity, gaps are created in terms of what identities are privileged and/or considered that interfere in creating more equitable and inclusive forms of instructional practices. It is precisely for this reason that representation matters when considering the creation of a team of instructional leaders, as we highlight in figure 5.1, in order to prevent gaps in identity orientation that create an incomplete picture of lived experiences.

In developing a team of inclusive instructional leaders who can provide culturally responsive instructional supervision, it is important to consider the visible and less-visible ways in which US society values identities that center power and privilege. In the ensuing sections of this chapter, race and

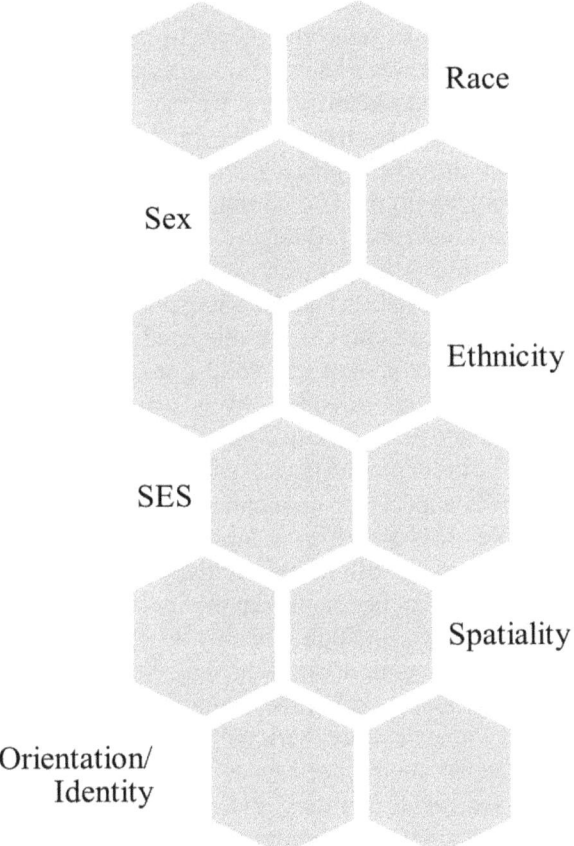

Race

Sex

Ethnicity

SES

Spatiality

Orientation/
Identity

Figure 5.1.   Societal Mosaic of Lived Experiences as It Relates to a Supervision Team

sex will be discussed to unpack how these identities are bedrocks of societal control in the United States. Following that, a section on various sociocultural identities to consider is provided to understand better how representation for instructional leaders goes beyond more visible identities.

SHIFTING AWAY FROM RACIAL
AND SEXUAL CONTRACTS

To engage in this work, educators can look to seminal pieces of literature that address how both race and sex are used to perpetuate inequities in US society. When looking at the history of the United States, one can easily see how both race and sex have been used to consolidate power and privilege in

White males. Look no further than the list of US presidents to see how these identities have been used to reinforce power in the United States—through 2020, there has been one US president who identifies as Black, and there have been no US presidents who identify as a woman. This has not occurred by chance—US society reinforces these social contracts.

In one of the more influential pieces of literature that addresses how racial inequities are perpetuated in the United States, Mills[4] writes about *the racial contract* that gives power and privilege to White citizens in almost every social construct possible. White citizens are allowed to live anywhere in the United States as their whiteness acts as a passport (spatial privilege), while Black and Native American citizens are relegated to urban areas (especially for Black citizens outside of the rural South) or to reservations (for Native Americans). Beyond spatial privilege, Mills discusses how White people benefit from social exclusion of those considered "subhuman."

People of color in the United States have long had to endure how White supremacy influences aspects of economic, political, and cultural control, specifically to people Mills describes as "nonwhite" (Black, Native American, Latinx, Asian American) or "off-white" (initially Irish, Jewish, and Italian).[5] Due to the legal treatment of people whom the social system does not identify as White (or white enough), including openly accepted and legally protected acts of enslavement, segregation, and lynching, Mills describes in detail the system of control that exists within the United States. Through this system, the United States devalues culture, heritage, and linguistic diversity.

At its core, the racial contract serves as a warning to White people who consider breaking the racial contract, and if they do, they too can be subjugated by those with power to hierarchical control. The United States has begun to see this process unfold through anti-CRT bills that prevent the discussion and instruction about the racialized history of the country. As Mills[6] describes, "[It is] hardly discussed in mainstream moral and political theory, that we live in a world which has been *foundationally shaped for the past five hundred years by the realities of European domination and the gradual consolidation of global white supremacy*" (p. 20).

Related to the fallacy of US society being postracial is the fallacy of the United States not being a patriarchal society. While women's rights (to varying degrees) have been protected through legal systems (such as the right to vote), Pateman[7] details how societal structures contribute to the oppression of women, specifically the subjugation of women and the inalienable patriarchal rights of men. Not only is feminism marginalized in US society, but civil freedoms are aligned with masculine attributes, and there remains an inordinate amount of "power that men exercise over women" (p. 1).

In her work, Pateman describes *the sexual contract*, one that challenges assumptions about the value society places on women and women's bodies.

Within US society (and Western society more broadly), Pateman argues the oppression of women is evident in social structures that allow their bodies to be seen as property and thus relegate their autonomy as individuals.[8] These societal structures—social contracts—reinforce patriarchal control, specifically through marriage and prostitution, which views women as sexual beings that are property to be controlled and reinforces patriarchal beliefs about women being subservient.

Increasingly, women's rights in the United States can be critiqued through Pateman's theory of the sexual contract. Access to safe and legal abortions—a right that should be a decision made by women for their own physical, mental, and emotional health—is increasingly being determined by state-level policies across the United States.[9] As such, Pateman[10] would argue that state and civil laws are inherently patriarchal, attempting to exert control over a woman's body in a subordinate manner, which mirrors that of control over the body of an enslaved person or what Pateman calls "a civil slave" (p. 15).

Traditional conceptions of race and birth sex are two visual identities in which educators can intentionally create a representative team of instructional leaders. However, there are also less visible identities that educators can and should consider when creating a diverse group of educators to help teachers reflect on instructional practices through supervision. In the section below, other sociocultural identities are illuminated to help develop a group of educators who will be better equipped to enact culturally responsive instructional supervision than a single, often White, administrator.

OTHER SOCIOCULTURAL IDENTITIES TO CONSIDER

In developing a team of leaders who can provide culturally responsive instructional supervision, it is important to consider the visible and less-visible ways US society values identities that center power and privilege. As previously discussed, race and sex are two identities that are bedrocks of societal privilege and thus control in the United States. However, there are other sociocultural identities that are critically important to consider when creating an inclusive team of educators who can provide feedback about instruction—one that centers marginalized identities in providing feedback about instruction, thus creating more inclusive learning communities.

Ethnicity

Ethnicity includes how groups of people are socially connected by language, cultural traditions, and religion, among other aspects. In US society, people who do not adhere to White and European traditions—such as speaking

English, celebrating cultural traditions that are considered "secular" (e.g., Columbus Day, St. Patrick's Day, how a birthday is celebrated), or sharing Christian-based beliefs—are otherized within US society. While there are more nuanced aspects of ethnicity to consider, language and cultural traditions play a huge role in the privileging of identities and how this is replicated in schools.

When considering how it is represented in the creation of a team of instructional supervisors, ethnicity can be embodied in a variety of ways, including but not limited to ensuring that

- Various spoken languages are seen as an asset and a sign of intelligence, which allows for multilanguage representation and moves away from deficit-oriented perceptions of students who speak English as an additional language in the classroom;
- Cultural traditions of all students are represented, not just those traditionally celebrated by White students in the United States, such as various ways people value and honor their ancestors, as well as how festivals and food are associated with celebrations; and
- Religious beliefs, specifically recognizing days of worship, are reflected when students are expected to be in school, including major holidays celebrated by Muslims and Jews and not just major Christian holidays.

Again, there are many more nuanced ways in which ethnicity can be defined and honored in a school system. However, for these identities to be more readily acknowledged, celebrated, and protected, a team of representative educators can and should be developed to expedite the development of culturally responsive instructional supervision and how feedback about pedagogical practices are provided. Doing so ensures that school systems see cultural and ethnic diversity as an asset, which is a key component of ensuring students and community members see themselves in the curriculum and through various instructional practices.

Socioeconomic Status or Class

Socioeconomic status (SES), or class, specifically in the capitalist US society, influences the way people think about wealth, the standard of living that wealth provides, and how the status of wealth either privileges or marginalizes people. In the United States, it is critically important that SES is not viewed in isolation from race, ethnicity, gender, or geography, as there is a complex and nuanced history of how the United States has privileged White, Anglo-Saxon men economically. However, SES does influence people differently in how they interact with education systems in the United States, *as well as* how people navigate their education to maintain or improve the privileges afford by class.

To ensure there is a team of inclusive leaders with a wide range of SES representation, school leaders should consider how SES influences the way people think about education, including but not limited to educators who might have experiences

- Receiving welfare support structures such as subsidized housing, heat assistance, medical assistance, or supplemental food assistance, as well as the lived experience of using any or all of these support structures as a child or a young adult;
- Disrupting beliefs about earned education level and the *societal perception* of status or prestige of a job based on societal beliefs (e.g., high school diploma and working in the food service industry; working in a trade such as an electrician, plumber, phlebotomist; or having a college degree to be an accountant or lawyer that affords privilege); and
- Understanding that wealth, especially intergenerational wealth, often is capable of transcending racial and ethnic differences, affording people from a wide variety of visible sociocultural identities to possibly find connections based on the lived experiences of navigating the capitalist US society that often otherizes those living in poverty.

Ensuring a team of educators who provide feedback on instructional practices have a wide variety of lived experiences based on SES is crucial if schools are to push past middle-class norms and deficit mindsets about education. To be clear, those with privileged SES identities can provide meaningful and powerful instruction to students who are not from privileged SES backgrounds. However, it takes deep reflection and learning from students and parents to understand different lived SES experiences. Understanding the role SES plays in how we approach instructional practices is especially important considering how a team is developed.

Spatiality

Understanding the role space and place plays on our own lived experiences is a direct result of the political and economic system reinforced by US society. As such, it is crucial for a representative team of instructional leaders to consider how and in what ways space influences the way we look at lived experiences of students, parents, and teachers. To do so, however, requires educators (and society more broadly) to understand that spatial identities are often otherized and marginalized by various groups, often resulting in political ideological influence that keeps people separated and lacking connection with one another.

When considering how spatiality can be considered within a team of instructional leaders, educators will want to consider how people view spatial identities, specifically stereotypes, including but not limited to

- Rural identities which often are associated with lower rates of education, high percentage of White populations in rural spaces outside of the rural South, and often the spatial isolation of cultural and social capital housed in urban areas;
- Suburban or town identities that have some social capital because of their proximity to urban areas but also tend to house racial and ethnic-specific population clusters that perpetuate de facto segregation seen in US school systems; and
- Urban or city identities that house large Black and Brown populations and are labeled as epicenters of high rates of crime, drug use, and extreme poverty, as well as concentrations of social, cultural, and political capital.

Many of these are misguided socialized stereotypes. For example, many well-educated rural children choose to leave rural areas because of the negative connotation of growing up rural coupled with the lack of access to cultural and economic opportunities that are housed in larger urban areas. Conversely, many urban children must combat the implication that their existence is defined by daily exposure to drugs and crime, or that access to social and cultural capital is not always available to them based on their race or ethnicity. Since spatiality matters—that the space we grow up in is part of our identity—it is important to consider this when creating a representative team.

Orientation/Identity

Sexual orientation and gender identity are less visible forms of how people identify who they are based on how they are attracted to others, as well as their internal sense of gender, both of which may or may not be expressed openly to others. In the United States, there is a long legal history of laws and policies that prevent people from openly expressing either orientation or identity, creating a troubling history for people who identify as part of the LGBTQIA+ community.

These issues of discrimination continue to this day in public schools. As a result, education systems create and reinforce policies that make it difficult for students who don't identify as heterosexual to see themselves in curriculum or instruction or for transgender students to use restrooms or participate on sports teams, among other structural challenges.

When school leaders consider developing a team of inclusive instructional leaders, orientation and identity can and should be centered by

- Including optional books for students to read that explore and normalize students who are part of the LGBTQIA+ community, especially as it relates to feeling minoritized, marginalized, or otherized due to societal stigma based on orientation and/or identity;
- Ensuring all students feel represented regarding orientation and identity, specifically in ways that are developmentally appropriate regarding curricula and observed instructional practices, as well as by collecting data about orientation and identity to ensure representation; and
- Encouraging educators who are part of the LGBTQIA+ community to be open, celebrate LGBTQIA+ moments in US history, and serve as role models for LGBTQIA+ youth, specifically to ensure various orientation and identity representation among teaching staff.[11]

It is important for a team of instructional leaders to have orientation and identity representation to be more aware and conscious of heteronormative beliefs and to combat antitrans policies and practices. As stated earlier, we believe that all educators can be allies to the LGBTQIA+ community, but to do so they must acknowledge how their identity and orientation privileges them in a society that openly discriminates against the LGBTQIA+ community. Ensuring that the team of instructional leaders considers these sociocultural identities is critical in providing more culturally responsive instruction for all children.

DETERMINING HOW "INSTRUCTIONAL SUCCESS" IS MEASURED

Once a representative team of instructional leaders has been developed for the purpose of providing feedback about instruction from a group with diverse perspectives, the team itself will need to be clear about communicating what "good instruction" looks like. Since the inception of NCLB, educators have continually been told a message that conflates high-quality instruction with student success. This is invalid for several reasons, most notably that good teaching is centered on pedagogical practices that encourage and promote higher-order thinking, which often directly conflicts with standardized testing that is inherently biased based on race, ethnicity, culture, and geography.

To move past these destructive paradigms that see students as vessels to fill and assume a deficit mindset about students, instructional leaders must work to define how culturally responsive instructional supervision can support teaching practices that acknowledge the assets and strengths that children bring with them to the classroom based on their sociocultural identities.

Working together, representative teams of teacher leaders can provide feedback about instructional practices that otherwise might go unseen or not reflected upon if feedback is only provided by one person—historically a White principal. As such, with time, feedback from a diverse team of instructional leaders expedites the development of teachers at the individual level to reflect on their own instruction and find ways to increase and improve culturally responsive teaching practices and student achievement.

When considering the definition of "instructional success" educators must be empowered to meet students where they are and engage them in meaningful questions about topics that matter to them and their respective lives. This means engaging in ongoing conversations, from a teacher leader to another teacher, about how and in what ways teachers develop a reflective stance about

- Pedagogical practices (How do lower-order thinking instructional practices scaffold higher-order thinking instructional practices, such as synthesizing, evaluating, critiquing, and creating once foundational knowledge has been acquired?);
- Equitable practices (How do instructional practices play out in the classroom—for example, are some children viewed as uncapable of certain learn activities because of poor standardized testing, ability grouping, racialized identity, multilanguage household, and so on—and is everyone given the opportunity to engage in deep and meaningful learning?); and
- Inclusion and belonging practices (how does the curriculum and the instruction provided in the classroom meet the sociocultural identities of students who can learn more about their own identities to better see themselves as members of US society as well as the identities of others that will help them to understand the need to create a more inclusive society that allows all people to feel like they are valued and belong?).

When teachers only focus on measuring student achievement on tests (and when they are actively reinforced by state and federal education systems that this is the only desired outcome), students are left behind. However, when teachers are supported by a group of diverse and represented peers, they can be provided feedback that expedites growth in culturally responsive teaching, asset-based mindsets, and instruction that empowers them to discuss and address social inequities. However, this cannot be accomplished through teacher evaluation models, but rather through ongoing formative feedback that honors growth, reflection, and celebrates new ways of thinking.

THE GOAL IS NOT TO MAINTAIN COMFORTABLENESS

If schools are to address the inequities of US society, educators will have to acknowledge, accept, and enact an education system that is neither ahistorical nor apolitical. As stated earlier, this does not mean that educators should be embarrassed by their privileged identities. What it does mean, however, is that school leaders and teachers alike must deeply reflect upon how their privileged identities play out in the enactment of the education they provide. Once educators acknowledge these privileges, they must then work tirelessly to make sure all students feel like they belong and receive a rigorous education to help them navigate an inequitable world.

As a result, the goal of a team of representative instructional leaders is to remember two outcomes, which interact with each other simultaneously and in parallel. One goal is to meet teachers where they are and support them in their development to provide more culturally responsive teaching. This means approaching feedback from a place of support if instruction is deemed culturally damaging or culturally destructive. While this might seem counterintuitive, many teachers are simply unaware of how their teaching comes across to others, and to grow they need feedback that sees them as imperfect humans attempting to improve an imperfect society.

The other goal is to directly point out how and when instruction yields culturally proficient outcomes, as well as when the outcomes are culturally destructive.[12] Nothing will change in US society if the instruction provided within the schoolhouse stays the same, and as such, there must be feedback from high-quality instructors with a wide variety of sociocultural identities to assist in this process. Validation and redirection are both required to reflect on how and in what ways culturally responsive teaching is conceptualized, considered, acculturated, and codified into practice. It is with this feedback that education systems can ensure all students receive instruction that honors their identities.

With all of this said, it is the responsibility of the representative instructional supervision team to support change not comfort. The work will be challenging on many levels, including what happens when a teacher repeatedly displays culturally damaging instructional practices. However, with the proper support and ongoing scaffolding, most people will grow due to discomfort or productive struggle because they ultimately care about the students they serve. It is the responsibility of the supervision team to communicate how feedback can be provided, what support structures are needed for development, and what data should be collected through observations and walkthroughs.

BEING CLEAR ABOUT STEPS FOR SUCCESS

To fully support the development of a CCRI, principals will need to flatten the hierarchy associated with instructional feedback and lean on the expertise of a variety of teacher leaders who possess a wide array of sociocultural identities. In turn, this representative team will play a large role in school improvement efforts, specifically centering the lived experiences of students who have minoritized, marginalized, and otherized identities and experiences. It is the opportunity to provide critique—not criticism—that is at the heart of culturally responsive instructional supervision.

Throughout the remainder of this book, principals and teacher leaders will be asked to consider what culturally responsive instructional supervision looks like in practice. Chapter 6 grounds the work by determining the goals for walkthroughs, specifically how to measure equity through instructional observations quantitatively. From these collaborative efforts, the representative teams of instructional supervisors can facilitate reflection about the data collected, as well as ensure staff are empowered to engage with the observation data to improve instructional practices and target ongoing professional development.

Most times teachers will be able to use formative feedback to improve instruction and make ongoing adjustments to improve equitable instruction for all students. However, it is also crucial that a team of teacher leaders providing feedback about instruction also has a plan for when instruction is considered culturally destructive. In chapter 7, educators are encouraged to define what teaching looks like when it lacks cultural responsiveness, as well as identify the types of feedback and cycles of inquiry that can be used to develop culturally responsive teaching that is seen as a tool for growth instead of a weapon of fear.

Once a feedback system is determined and implemented in practice, learning should occur beyond the feedback provided by the representative team of instructional leaders. Chapter 8 addresses how teachers can grow individually and use self-reflection as an ongoing tool to drive instructional improvement efforts. Chapter 9 addresses ways to develop in small critical colleague groups of a few peers to determine growth goals, deepen understanding of equity, and challenge taken-for-granted assumptions. Chapter 10 supports the development of peer observations to dismantle inequitable outcomes and support teachers and students.

As stated previously, there is no quick answer for this work. However, school systems can produce more equitable outcomes for students when the right supports are in place and when teachers are empowered to be part of the solution. Because of this precise reason, the remainder of this book focuses on how feedback from a diverse instructional supervision team can prevent opportunity gaps. Further, feedback from this perspective and intention offers hope to all educators—regardless of their sociocultural identities—empowering them to make a difference in how US society becomes more equitable and inclusive.

NOTES

1. Irby, D. J. (2021). *Stuck improving: Racial equity and school leadership.* Harvard Education Press.

2. Kendi, I. X. (2021). Our new postracial myth. *The Atlantic.*

3. Schwartz, S. (2021). 8 states debate bills to restrict how teachers discuss racism, sexism. *Education Week.* https://www.edweek.org/policy-politics/8-states-debate-bills-to-restricthow-teachers-discuss-racism-sexism/2021/04

4. Mills, C. W. (1997). *The racial contract.* Cornell University Press.

5. Mills, C. W. (1997). *The racial contract.* Cornell University Press.

6. Mills, C. W. (1997). *The racial contract.* Cornell University Press.

7. Pateman, C. (1998). *The sexual contract.* Stanford University Press.

8. Pateman, C. (1998). *The sexual contract.* Stanford University Press.

9. Bustillo, X. (2022). Who and what is behind abortion ban trigger law bills? Two groups laid the groundwork. *National Public Radio.* https://www.npr.org/2022/07/08/1110299496/trigger-laws-13-states-two-groups-laid-groundwork

10. Pateman, C. (1998). *The sexual contract.* Stanford University Press.

11. Duarte, B. J. (2020). Forced back into the closet: A (queer) principal's attempt to maintain queer erasure. *Journal of Cases in Educational Leadership, 23*(4), 20–34.

12. Cormier, D. R. (2022). Prototyping the Cultural Proficiency Continuum Dialogic Protocol with professional development school teacher interns. *Urban Education.* https://doi.org/10.1177/00420859221140405; and Lindsey, R. B., Robins, K. N., & Terrell, R. D. (2009). *Cultural proficiency: A manual for school leaders.* Corwin.

Chapter 6

Working Together to Determine What Culturally Responsive Instructional Supervision Looks Like

Once a representative group of teacher leaders with instructional leadership experience has been selected, the real work to provide culturally responsive instructional supervision begins. It is one thing to make sure that a group of educators with diverse racial and ethnic backgrounds and sociocultural identities are selected to provide feedback about culturally responsive teaching—it is completely another challenge to influence and empower others to shift their approach to ensure they provide culturally responsive instruction to all children. However, education systems can make critical shifts in how they support the development of teachers, and they can do so in several different ways.

One of the biggest challenges facing a school system that wants to support the ongoing development of culturally responsive teaching will be transitioning away from the traditional supervision model of principal providing feedback to teachers. With the creation of accountability practices, many educators have been conditioned to believe that principals—people with hierarchical power—are instructional leaders, and often this is simply not the case. To be clear, principals can be instructional leaders, but often there are many other instructional leaders among teachers who can provide expert advice on how to improve instruction.[1]

There are also many benefits to shifting the feedback process from a hierarchical approach to one that empowers all teachers, at all developmental stages, to take charge in the development of their own critical consciousness.[2] When a school is able to develop a CCRI, teachers learn to look to teacher leaders and to each other to develop instruction that is inclusive and immediately applicable to the classroom. It is through the cocreation of knowledge and learning from peers that educators can deeply question systemic inequities and how a school system can learn together and be accountable to the communities they serve and not to deficit-based assessment models.

As such, educators engaged in facilitating culturally responsive instructional supervision must continue to shift education from a paradigm of high-stakes accountability and testing to one that employs instructional supervision practices that are inclusive, asset-based, and loving and accommodating of all children. To accomplish this change in how educators view their roles in education, teachers must be provided ongoing opportunities for feedback about how their instruction is inclusive (or not) and then be provided the opportunity to reflect on how to promote greater inclusion and equity. One of the quickest ways to accomplish this is through the ongoing collection of observational data.

DETERMINING GOALS FOR WALKTHROUGHS

Before a team of supervisors starts providing feedback through walkthroughs, several norms and purposeful outcomes must be decided upon first. Much of our work in this chapter is influenced by the framework of the Instructional Practices Inventory (IPI).[3] To be considered an influential practice, walkthroughs should be quick observations that last no more than five minutes, are unannounced to prevent "dog and pony shows" for teacher observations, and should be used to provide feedback to the teacher prior to the end of the day.[4] If that is not possible, feedback should be given no later than 24 hours after the walkthrough. In doing so, walkthroughs can occur throughout the day to create a culture of ongoing improvement about instruction.

Using collated data to provide snapshots of instruction during different periods or time intervals (e.g., week, month, quarter), the team of representative instructional supervisors can provide insight into what is occurring within the school building at any given time. It can be assumed that a member of the instructional supervision team could collect four different observations each day, meaning that a team of five teacher leaders could collect 20 observations a day and 100 observations in a week.[5] That means 120 days of instruction (time removed for testing and other noninstructional days) could produce upward of 2,400 points of observation data in a school year.

When thinking about how walkthroughs are perceived, the data collected from the observations should be a form of formative feedback used to support growth rather than "gotcha" practices.[6] Part of what walkthroughs can accomplish is a feedback structure that helps teachers by holding up a figurative mirror to answer questions about how culturally responsive instruction is being implemented. What was observed regarding pedagogical practices?

How was equity visibly seen by an outsider entering the classroom? How might students feel they belong as a result of their perceived learning and achievement? How were their identities represented in the classroom?

Walkthroughs should also result in data that can be collected, reviewed, and analyzed at the individual level, in small groups, and at the school level.[7] Part of developing culturally responsive instructional supervision practices is to ensure that educators have evidence to look at, question, and use to improve quality of instruction, as opposed to only being concerned about achievement data. One of the explicit goals of walkthroughs is to provide teachers with deep insights on how their teaching affects student learning processes, which includes providing constructive feedback aimed at creating culturally responsive instructional outcomes that directly connect to the lived experiences of the students.

As such, when considering how to implement culturally responsive instructional supervision, the most important feedback walkthroughs can provide is the focus on how to increase equitable outcomes for learning experiences. Achievement is clearly important—every teacher wants their students to be academically successful. However, to ensure that outcome, teachers must continually think about—and be given feedback on—the degree to which equitable and inclusive outcomes occur in their classrooms as a result of culturally responsive teaching practices.

WHAT DOES EQUITY DATA LOOK LIKE IN A WALKTHROUGH?

As teams conduct walkthroughs with the focus of providing culturally responsive instructional supervision, there should be a clear focus on what the "look fors" are in the process. While not exhaustive, the following section provides an overview of what *can* be looked for and how data can be collected to determine if equitable and inclusive instruction is occurring throughout a school building. In short, walkthroughs should be based on observations to support "have you thought of" feedback.

The walkthrough data sheets provided in this chapter *exemplify what instructional leaders might develop*, which have been informed by processes like the IPI.[8] They should not be considered the only types of data that can be collected to reflect on culturally responsive teaching practices. They are, however, informed by the eight principles of culturally responsive teaching established by Geneva Gay,[9] and as such, culturally responsive instructional supervision should be aligned to her tenets. Practitioners can and should think of other categories to consider regarding what is important to their school building to support culturally responsive teaching.

Pedagogical Principles

Equitable instruction starts with the idea and belief that learning should be multidimensional and provides students with appropriate scaffolding to engage in a wide variety of learning opportunities. Providing students with the opportunity to go from low-order thinking to higher-order thinking learning strategies requires instructors to deeply engage in reflection about what they believe students are capable of learning.

Culturally responsive teaching also requires instructors to consider *how* they are applying their knowledge in their learning. While it is not bad to start with instruction that helps students remember and understand concepts, over time educators should focus on increasing instructional practices that allow students to apply and analyze information and eventually evaluate and create to show deep understanding.

Related is how educators apply culturally responsive teaching strategies to encourage a deep understanding of knowledge. At times it is reasonable for students to engage in worksheet-based learning, but educators should also think about using teacher-led lectures, which allows for questions and answers, as well as student-led work and activities.[10] This can also be accomplished through instructional practices that provide teacher-led exploration (class-wide or in smaller groups), student-led exploration of a new concept, or student-led creation of a product that shows deep comprehension of the learning objective.

Another observable concept of culturally responsive teaching can be noted in how questions posed by students are incorporated into the lesson, as well as how they can be used to deepen thinking and understanding. In some classrooms, especially at the high school level or in classes that deal with the pressure of covering material assessed on standardized tests, questions are not always observed because of the pace of instruction, or they are not used to deepen contextual understanding and metacognition. For culturally responsive teaching to occur, educators need to reflect on how questions can be used to deepen both individual and classroom understanding more broadly.

As stated previously, the quality of pedagogy provided by educators is an issue of equity, particularly as the United States has a history of dumbing down instruction and providing learning opportunities that approach historically marginalized students with a deficit-based mindset. Due to this history, it is critical for instructional leaders to engage in culturally responsive instructional supervision that provides feedback to teachers about the rigor of pedagogy to ensure all students can engage in higher-order learning structures and opportunities.

With a focus on rigorous pedagogy—not standardized achievement—students can be provided with the tools to critique, question, and engage in action that addresses inequities. Table 6.1 provides an example of a walk-through data sheet that culturally responsive instructional supervisors might use in their data collection process. At the bottom of the sheet are the three pedagogical principles previously discussed, namely (1) multidimensional learning, (2) application of knowledge, and (3) student questions. Within these principles are ranked-ordered continuums to note what is observed and how to quickly enter that into the data sheet example. The data sheet example also provides instructional supervisors the opportunity to scribe additional observation notes.

Creating a Reflective and Inclusive Community of Learning

While ensuring rigorous pedagogical principles are being used in classrooms, it is also important that teachers provide feedback about what is being learned to empower students to create a reflective and inclusive learning environment. Culturally responsive teaching must consider how student voice is considered[11] when creating an inclusive learning environment.

Classrooms where only a few students are expected to share their voice—often based on assumptions about intelligence, ability to pay attention, or connection to the topic being taught—are neither inclusive nor engaging. Culturally responsive teaching finds ways to increase a variety of students' voices over time, with the expectation that students will share their understanding in ways that honor their voice, their sociocultural identities, and the cultural assets they bring to the classroom.[12] As such, these should be measurable and observable instructional practices.

When considering how to observe what a reflective and inclusive community of learning looks like, culturally responsive instructional supervision teams can also help observe how teachers provide opportunities for comprehension checks. Historically, teachers make the faulty assumption that students do not need to ask clarifying questions if they came to class, or that questions asked during lecture-based instruction is sufficient to ensure understanding.

As teachers think about equitable concepts of checking for understanding, teachers can use exit slips or tickets and small group checks before the end of class. At the heart of this effort is the attempt to ensure support structures occur for understanding based on providing comprehension checks that meet the sociocultural needs of individual students.

Related to this, teachers need support to develop culturally responsive teaching practices by focusing on feedback that is validating and affirming to students. Historically, many approaches to instruction have only focused on feedback that address the underlying learning objective and fail to make

Table 6.1 Pedagogical Principles Walkthrough Data Sheet Example

Date	Time	Grade	Teacher	Subject	Multidimensional Learning	Application of Knowledge	Student Questions	Observation Notes
10/3	10:31	7	Yang	Science	(1) remember/ understand	(2) teacher-led lecture	(2) questions addressed but not used to deepen contextual understanding	Teacher was engaged in a lecture where students were taking notes on the scientific method
10/3	10:39	6	Ndessokia	Technology	(2) apply/ analyze	(4) teacher-led exploration	(3) questions seen as a way to deepen individual understanding	Teacher was modeling for students how to consider creating a robot that could be programed to perform a basic function with students asking clarifying questions
10/3	10:52	8	Parker	Math	(1) remember/ understand	(3) student-led board work	(4) questions used as a way to deepen collective understanding	Teacher was asking students to come to the board and model how to solve problems, with students asking questions about accuracy of solutions
10/3	11:04	8	Harris	Social Studies	(3) evaluate/ create	(5) student-led exploration	(3) questions seen as a way to deepen individual understanding	Teacher was supporting students as they engaged in an exploration-based activity asking them to evaluate the impact of the Monroe Doctrine on colonization

Date	Time	Grade	Teacher	Subject	Multidimensional Learning	Application of Knowledge	Student Questions	Observation Notes
10/4	10:28	7	Flores	English	(3) evaluate/create	(6) student-led creative product	(3) questions seen as a way to deepen individual understanding	Teacher was conducting a writer's workshop and meeting with students individually about their personal narrative of their family's history
10/4	10:37	6	Grant	Spanish	(1) remember/understand	(1) individual worksheet-based	(1) questions not observed	Teacher was grading papers at their desk while students sat quietly completing vocabulary sheets

Multidimensional Learning: (1) remember/understand; (2) apply/analyze; (3) evaluate/create

Application of Knowledge: (1) individual worksheet-based; (2) teacher-led lecture; (3) student-led board work; (4) teacher-led exploration; (5) student-led exploration; (6) student-led creative product; (7) other

Student Questions: (1) questions not observed; (2) questions addressed but not used to deepen contextual understanding; (3) questions seen as a way to deepen individual understanding; (4) questions used as a way to deepen collective understanding

deeper connections to the home life or cultural understanding of each student. As teachers progress through their development of providing culturally responsive teaching, they must learn how to make broad but nuanced cultural connections based on the sociocultural identities of each student, but also, they must strive to deeply understand the complexity of each student's lived experience.

Finding ways to make a reflective and inclusive learning community into observable practices can be challenging. However, these are measurable aspects of culturally responsive teaching that can be valued through supervision practices and increased with implementation over time. Honoring student voices and identities, as well as the cultural assets they bring to a learning community, is critical for inclusion and belonging.

Additionally, ensuring students have a deep understanding of what is being taught through feedback that is validating and affirming are core concepts of culturally responsive teaching that can and should be measured for purposes of teachers reflecting on instructional practices. Table 6.2 provides a second example of a walkthrough data sheet that culturally responsive instructional supervisors might use in their data collection process. At the bottom of the sheet are the three aspects of creating a reflective and inclusive community of learning previously discussed, namely (1) student voice, (2) checking for comprehension, and (3) validating and affirming feedback. Within these principles are ranked-ordered continuums to note what is observed and how to quickly enter that into the data sheet example. Again, this data sheet example provides instructional supervisors the opportunity to scribe additional observation notes.

Emancipatory and Liberating Instruction

At the core of culturally responsive teaching is the idea of providing meaningful instruction that can be emancipatory and liberating for all students in the classroom. To accomplish this, culturally responsive instructional supervision can collect data on the degree to which a lesson empowers students to address inequities they witness or experience in their own lives. Historically, education in the United States has attempted to make learning contextless, ahistorical, or apolitical;[13] however, culturally responsive teaching can be observed to acknowledge bias in the United States and empower students to think about *and* enact change.

Culturally responsive teaching should be able to provide differentiated instruction based on sociocultural identities and asset-based approaches to learning. This requires teachers to receive support from instructional supervisors to consider and increase awareness of sociocultural identities as well as those identities that are privileged within the US schooling context. The

Table 6.2 Reflective and Inclusive Community of Learning Walkthrough Data Sheet Example

Date	Time	Grade	Teacher	Subject	Student Voice	Checking for Comprehension	Validating and Affirming Feedback	Observation Notes
1/28	1:03	3	Thomas	Math	(2) a variety of students share their voice	(4) small group check	(3) connects learning objective to broad cultural identities	Teacher used an exploration strategy to see if students could teach each other tally marks and tables to count classroom votes based on worksheet
1/28	1:15	3	Salzberg	Math	(3) students will participate at some point to honor voice, identity, and strengths offered	(4) small group check	(4) learning objective connected to cultural identities and personalized lived experiences	Teacher used an exploration strategy to see if students could teach each other tally marks and tables to count classroom votes about their favorite foods
1/29	1:05	4	Wheeler	ELA	(1) only a few students share their voice	(1) no check	(1) no connection to learning objective	Teacher was lecturing about how to create a constructed response—there was no pausing to check for comprehension and students did not appear to know the objective
1/29	1:14	4	Campbell	ELA	(2) a variety of students share their voice	(5) individualized support	(3) connects learning objective to broad cultural identities	Teacher was reviewing the objective about creating a constructed response and asked students to write about the importance of family traditions—teacher provided individual support

Table 6.2 (continued)

Date	Time	Grade	Teacher	Subject	Student Voice	Checking for Comprehension	Validating and Affirming Feedback	Observation Notes
1/29	1:25	5	Doughty	Social Studies	(1) only a few students share their voice	(2) lecture-based questions	(2) addresses the learning objective	Teacher was reviewing different types of government and asking students questions as they lectured
1/29	1:36	5	Williams	Social Studies	(2) a variety of students share their voice	(3) exit slip	(3) connects learning objective to broad cultural identities	Teacher was engaged in a form of Socratic seminar and made connections about the different types of governments throughout the world

Student Voice: (1) expectation that only a few students will share their voice; (2) expectation that a variety of students will share their voice; (3) expectation that all students will participate at some point to honor their voice, sociocultural identities, and strengths they offer

Checking for Comprehension: (1) no check; (2) lecture-based questions; (3) exit slip; (4) small group check; (5) individualized support

Validating and Affirming Feedback: (1) no connection to learning objective, (2) addresses understanding of learning objective; (3) addresses understanding of learning objective and broad cultural identities; (4) addresses understanding of learning objective, cultural identities, and personalized lived experience

highest form of culturally responsive teaching that can observed is when an educator provides the opportunity for a student to deeply reflect upon the role of individuals who reflect their sociocultural identities in society, and ultimately, to deeply reflect on their sociocultural identities and construction of the self to progress to a full and meaningful life.[14]

In addition to thinking about how to structure lessons that are culturally responsive, teachers can also reflect on the physical characteristics of their classroom and how it is intentionally representative to ensure all students feel included and have a sense of belonging. To be intentionally inclusive, teachers should consider if there are mostly Eurocentric representations, some observed student identities that are representative, or if many or all visible and nonvisible student identities are intentionally represented in the classroom.

Table 6.3 provides a third example of a walkthrough data sheet that culturally responsive instructional supervisors could use in their data collection process. At the bottom of the sheet are the three aspects of emancipatory and liberating instruction previously discussed, namely (1) empowerment to address inequities, (2) humanistic understanding of society and self, and (3) physical representation of identities in learning. Within these principles are ranked-ordered continuums to note what is observed and how to quickly enter that into the data sheet example. Again, this data sheet example provides instructional supervisors the opportunity to scribe any additional observations noted in the walkthrough process.

HOW ONGOING INSTRUCTIONAL
REFLECTIONS INFORM PRACTICE

When considering how to create, foster, and develop a community of culturally responsive instructors (CCRI), educational leaders should consider the purpose of data that is collected through culturally responsive instructional supervision walkthroughs. No one likes to be audited—think about the fear the word *audit* elicits.

Auditing an educator makes them feel defensive when they already exist in a society that, by and large, does not support teachers. If we audit educators, they ask themselves, "Did I do something wrong? What if I submitted something the wrong way? What consequences will I have to pay if someone else determines I was wrong or negligent?"

Instead, leaders implementing a culturally responsive instructional supervision process should frame the work as focusing on regular instructional reflections that can drive ongoing improvement efforts. This is an effort that requires love and support of educators—not casting blame. Through the

Table 6.3 Emancipatory and Liberating Instruction Walkthrough Data Sheet example

Date	Time	Grade	Teacher	Subject	Empowerment to Address Inequities	Humanistic Understanding of Society/Self	Physical Representation of Ethical Learning	Observation Notes
4/19	11:01	9	Pierce	English	(2) acknowledgment of bias	(2) acknowledgment of the role of privileged identities	(4) visible and nonvisible identities represented	Teacher was discussing *To Kill a Mockingbird* and the discriminatory legal system; student work and wide array of identities covered the walls
4/19	11:15	9–12	James	Industrial Tech.	(1) contextless learning	(1) lack of sociocultural awareness	(1) no student representation present	Teacher was having students build a birdhouse and there was no observed discussion of connection to society; no student work or identities represented on walls
4/19	11:25	10	Walker	Social Studies	(1) contextless learning	(1) lack of sociocultural awareness	(2) mostly or all Eurocentric representation	Teacher was discussing the Trail of Tears from the perspective of US policy of the 1830s; walls decorated with mostly White politicians

Date	Time	Grade	Teacher	Subject	Empowerment to Address Inequities	Humanistic Understanding of Society/Self	Physical Representation of Ethical Learning	Observation Notes
4/20	11:03	9 & 10	Lawrence	Geometry	(3) acknowledg-ment of bias	(3) reflecting on the role of sociocultural identities in society	(4) visible and nonvisible identities represented	Teacher asked class to calculate area of zip codes with 80% or more of people of color; discussion ensued about redlining; student work and wide array of identities on the walls
4/20	11:14	9-12	Beckwith	Physical Education	(3) empowerment to think about change	(3) reflecting on the role of sociocultural identities in society	(3) some observed representations of student identities	Teacher led team building activity requiring groups of various identities to reach a goal; questions were asked about the role of identity in learning to relate to one another
4/20	11:27	11	Hayward	English	(4) empowerment to enact change	(4) reflecting on the role of sociocultural identities on the self	(4) visible and nonvisible identities represented	Teacher had assigned term paper on understanding the role of identities in the US based on a favorite author

Empowerment to Address Inequities: (1) contextless learning; (2) acknowledgement of bias; (3) acknowledgement of privileged identities; (4) empowerment to think about change; (4) empowerment to enact change

Humanistic Understanding of Society/Self: (1) lack of sociocultural awareness; (2) acknowledgement of sociocultural identities in society; (3) reflecting on the role of sociocultural identities in society; (4) deeply reflecting on sociocultural identities of the self

Physical Representation of Identities within Learning: (1) no student representation present; (2) mostly or all Eurocentric representations given student identities; (3) some observed representations given student identities; (4) many visible and nonvisible sociocultural identities represented

data collection process, teams of instructional leaders can establish a culture where data about instruction is valued and wanted. At the heart of this work is to focus on regular instructional reflections that lead to improved culturally responsive teaching as well as improved outcomes for all students, especially those who are marginalized, minoritized, or otherized in school and the larger society.

It is from a variety of data collection sources that educators are able to learn about what is working for them and how they might learn from each other. *To be clear, the process is not an evaluative one, nor should it be used for human resource decisions.* The process of collecting and reviewing the data is to facilitate and engage in formative conversations that can drive learning with the individual teacher, with trusted peers, in small groups, and at the school-building level.

With enough data, faculty can take snapshots of walkthrough data collected over ten-minute periods of observations and make conclusions about what occurs on a regular basis in the schoolhouse. It is from this work that improvement efforts are made and professional development opportunities are identified. In short, a school doesn't get better by teachers just working alone and in isolation.

THE PROCESS OF EXAMINING WALKTHROUGH DATA

If we want educators to engage in the change process of developing their abilities to provide culturally responsive teaching, instructional leaders must empower teachers to make their own conclusions about the collected data. This means that the growth and development of educators will take time and patience, with a healthy tension (i.e., productive struggle) of what the representative instructional supervision team collects through walkthroughs and how the entire group of educators in a school building interprets the data. However, change takes the deepest root when it comes from the ground up, and data about culturally responsive practices will inform instructional improvement.

Working together, the team of representative instructional supervisors should collate and present information to the faculty based on the walkthrough data. This can be done in a variety of ways, including but not limited to schoolwide, grade level, and subject area data. Names of teachers should never be displayed in a public meeting but should be made available to the individual teacher if they would like to see their data and analyze it over the course of a quarter, a semester, or a school year.

Again, the data should never be used as a weapon or for summative purposes. Data is available to speak to the teacher about how they can best reflect on their practices to teach their students and what they might do to reflect upon and improve those teaching practices.

With the incredible amount of data available to review, reflect upon, and use as a springboard for improvement efforts, teachers can answer critical questions in and around culturally responsive teaching practices. With upward of 100 walkthrough data points collected by the representative supervision team each week, schools should have no short supply of data points to reflect upon, as noted in frameworks such as the IPI.[15]

For example, in figure 6.1, supervision teams could share data collected that details the extent to which students are engaged in their application of knowledge. By examining pedagogical practices, teachers could begin to ask themselves how to move away from individual worksheet-based instruction and increase student-led board work or student-led exploration activities. Over time, teachers learn how to reflect on the data and take charge of what instructional practices might occur at any given point in time during a walkthrough.

When reflecting on pedagogical principles, educators can reflect on other questions about instruction practices. Looking at multidimensional learning, how and to what extent are students being asked to remember or understand, apply or analyze, and evaluate or create? Thinking about the use of student questions, how are student questions or concerns observed in classroom

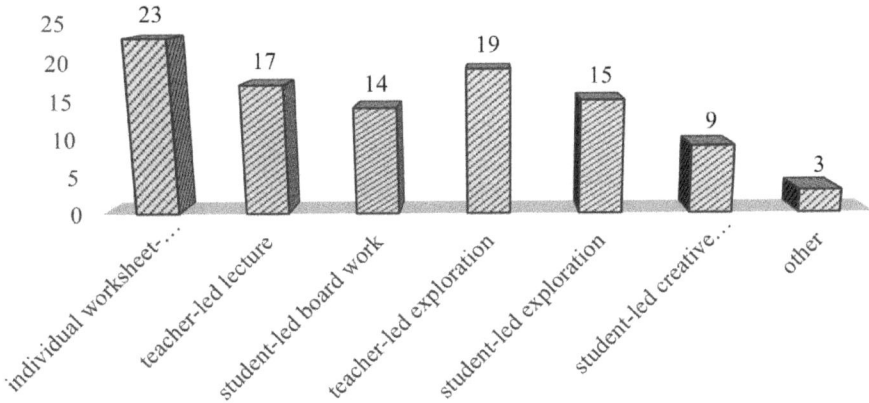

Figure 6.1. Application of Knowledge Chart Example

instruction, and are they used to deepen both individual and collective understanding?

These are the types of questions that can be asked through the collection of walkthrough data that targets and pinpoints pedagogical principles of instruction. Specifically, instructional leaders will want to review and reflect upon the quality of pedagogy provided by educators for students with historically marginalized identities.

To support and develop reflective and inclusive learning communities, educators should also continually reflect on instructional practices and ensure high levels of comprehension. Figure 6.2 provides collated data to analyze the degree to which classrooms provide validating and affirming feedback. This is critical in culturally responsive teaching practices because it asks how teachers might move beyond simply addressing the learning objective and move towards practices that make broad and nuanced cultural connections endemic to students' lived experiences.

It is the operationalizing of data collection—specifically the degree to which culturally responsive teaching practices can create a reflective and inclusive community of learning—that is critical to the feedback process about observed instructional practices. Teachers must also be able to reflect on data that considers the degree to which student voice is considered, particularly the notion that all students' voices matter, as well as the sociocultural identities and individual strengths students bring to the classroom.

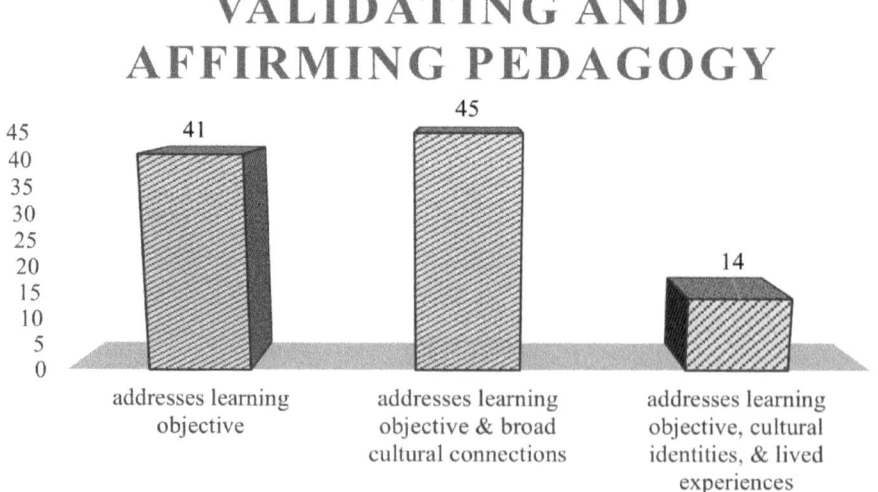

VALIDATING AND AFFIRMING PEDAGOGY

Figure 6.2. Validating and Affirming Feedback Chart Example

Additionally, teachers need to be able to check for comprehension in a way that supports students at the small group level as well as at the individual level. These are central, concretized components of culturally responsive teaching practices.

Ultimately, the goal of a team of representative instructional supervisors is to provide feedback about instructional practices that allow educators to reflect upon the degree to which their teaching is emancipatory and liberating. Figure 6.3 illustrates how data might be collected through walkthroughs that detail how students are empowered to address inequities they see and experience in their own lives. Examining data like this allows teachers to consider the degree to which they do or do not acknowledge bias is US society, and how students might enact change through their learning.

To create instruction that is emancipatory and liberating, teachers should also consider other aspects of their approaches to teaching. Data about the physical representation of ethical learning helps teachers reflect on how visible and less-visible sociocultural identities are represented in the room, including but not limited to representations of race, ethnicity, and identity/ orientation, among others.

This is directly tied to how students are supported to develop a humanistic understanding of society and the self, and how these understandings can lead to learning that increases awareness of how to create a more inclusive society.

EMPOWERMENT TO ADDRESS INEQUITIES

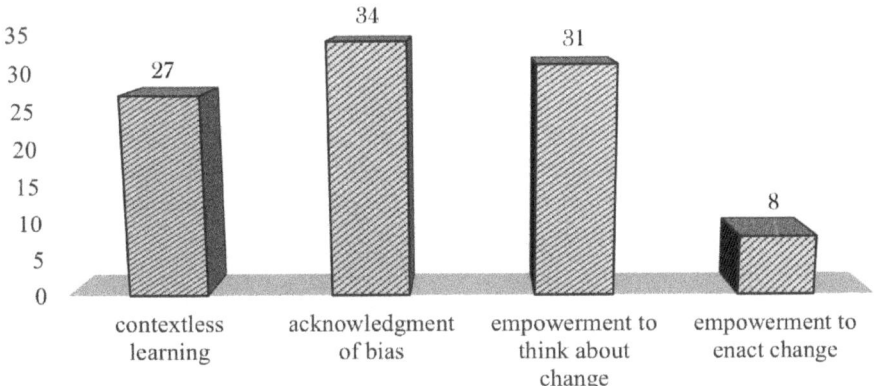

Figure 6.3.   Empowerment to Address Inequities Chart Example

HUMANISTIC UNDERSTANDING OF SOCIETY & SELF

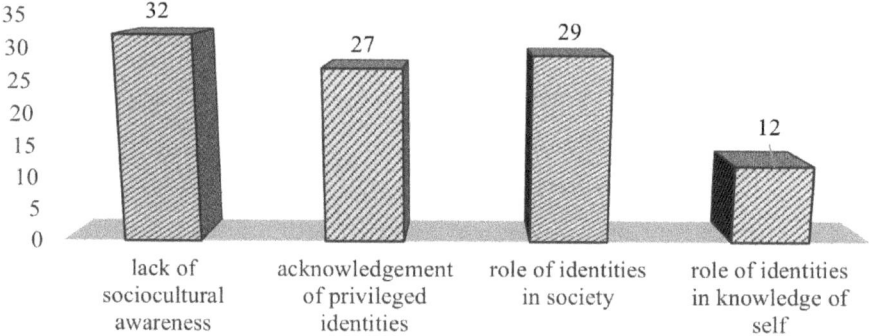

Figure 6.4. Humanistic Understanding of Society/Self Chart Example

Figure 6.4 provides an example of how this data might be observed and collected through walkthroughs.

USING DATA TO DRIVE PROFESSIONAL DEVELOPMENT EFFORTS

From ongoing collection and examination of walkthrough data, teachers, teacher leaders, and principals should be able to make data-informed decisions about how to improve equitable outcomes for students. To be clear, it is the process of collecting data from a diverse and representative group of teacher leaders with a strong focus on high-quality instructional practices that provide a foundation of trustworthiness to the work. Additionally, the intent of the process—the collection of walkthrough data—is not for evaluation purposes, but rather for formative feedback on how to operationalize the improvement of culturally responsive teaching practices.

It is from the reflection of data that teachers can have a hand in selecting improvement processes that target professional development efforts. Together, teachers, teacher leaders, and principals can ask questions in meaningful ways on how to improve culturally responsive teaching practices, including:

Pedagogical Principles

- Why is it important for all children to experience a wide range of multidimensional learning, including learning experiences that allow students to evaluate and create products based on what they have learned? What does applicable research say about how to increase multidimensional learning?
- How might we conceptualize teaching that moves from low-order application of knowledge and increase higher-order application of knowledge that focuses on exploration-based learning activities and student-led creative products that are tied to experiences of those marginalized, minoritized, and otherized in the United States? What sort of scaffolding is needed to launch exploration-based learning strategies?
- What ways might we be more aware of how to answer student questions that move past deficit-based mindsets and see questions as a way to honor strength-based approaches to instruction that deepen both individual and collective understanding? What is the prevailing thought on how to implement strength-based approaches to high-quality instruction?

Reflective and Inclusive Community of Learning

- Whose voices do we value in the classroom, and how might we move toward a collective expectation that all students will participate in some way, shape, or form in a manner that honors their voice, their sociocultural identities, and the strengths they offer as individuals? Is there a teacher in the school that already does this well, and are they willing to share what they know?
- How do we check for comprehension in a way that does not make assumptions about cultural norms and ensures learning occurs through small group checks and individual support structures? Would this be of interest for funding at the district level if other schools were interested in joining in professional development?
- What approaches can teachers take to ensure they provide validating and affirming feedback to students that not only addresses a learning objective, but does it in a manner that centers cultural identities and personalized lived experiences? Is there a practitioner-friendly article or newly printed book that can be used to form a book club?

Emancipatory and Liberating Instruction

- How do we empower students to address inequities they observe and experience in a way that not only acknowledges bias, but also empowers them to think about *and* enact change in their community? Is there an academic at a local university or a community activist that is willing to come and give a one-hour seminar?

- What reflection might need to take place among teachers to acknowledge the role of sociocultural identities in US society, embed this within instruction, and use this to drive learning about sociocultural identities of the self? What resources are readily available for teachers to read and engage with in small learning groups?
- Who is represented in the physical makeup of the classroom, including but not limited to what is honored, valued, and celebrated on classroom walls and how this is represented in visible and less-visible sociocultural identities? What classrooms in the school or in the district might be visited and observed that already have a high level of inclusion?

From these reflections, teams of educators can begin to target and pinpoint what professional development is needed to move instructional practices forward. It might be that professional development is something that can be offered locally by a fellow teacher who has an area of expertise and can share that in a professional development day or during an after-school teachers' meeting. It could also be that additional resources are needed, either across the district or from the district level. However, many of the answers are already available—it often is simply a matter of valuing what is measured and then ensuring what is valued becomes implemented.

This chapter offers a lot of information and suggestions. However, the ideas are neither complex nor are they set in stone. Teams of teachers need to determine what is valued, set up an observation schedule to measure what is valued through walkthroughs, and provide the data in a manner that can be easily analyzed by groups of teachers.

To be clear, this doesn't have to happen across an entire faculty—it can happen in grade-level teams, departments, and PLCs based on other organizational structures. However, it is the formative nature of the data that is valuable, namely, the ability to reflect upon what is going well and what can be improved upon, that leads to change in instructional practices.

The next chapter provides an overview of how instructional supervision might inform a plan of action and support for when instruction is observed to not be inclusive or culturally responsive. This includes defining what is culturally damaging or culturally destructive about the instructional practice, determining the feedback that is necessary to improve self-awareness and increase cultural responsiveness, and how to grow from the process. Ultimately, this type of feedback has to focus on the concept of growth rather than feedback being used as a weapon of fear.

NOTES

1. Ezzani, M. D. (2019). Principal and teacher instructional leadership: A cultural shift. *International Journal of Educational Management, 34*(3), 576–585.

2. Waite, S. R. (2021). Towards a theory of critical consciousness: A new direction for the development of instructional and supervisory leaders. *Journal of Educational Supervision, 4*(2), 65–79. https://doi.org/10.31045/jes.4.2.4

3. Valentine, J. (2009). *The instructional practices inventory: Using a student learning assessment to foster organizational learning.* National Staff Development Council, Annual Convention, St. Louis, MO.

4. Kachur, D. S., Stout, J. A., & Edwards, C. L. (2013). *Classroom walkthroughs to improve teaching and learning* (2nd ed.). Routledge.

5. Valentine, J. (2009). *The instructional practices inventory: Using a student learning assessment to foster organizational learning.* National Staff Development Council, Annual Convention, St. Louis, MO.

6. Moss, C. M., Brookhart, S. M., & Long, B. A. (2013). Administrators' roles in helping teachers use formative assessment information. *Applied Measurement in Education, 26*(3), 205–218.

7. Stoll, L., Bolam, R., McMahon, A., Wallace, M., & Thomas, S. (2006). Professional learning communities: A review of the literature. *Journal of Educational Change, 7*, 221–258.

8. Valentine, J. (2009). *The instructional practices inventory: Using a student learning assessment to foster organizational learning.* National Staff Development Council, Annual Convention, St. Louis, MO.

9. Gay, G. (2018). *Culturally responsive teaching: Theory, research, and practice* (2nd ed.). Teachers College Press.

10. Krathwohl, D. R. (2002). A revision of Bloom's taxonomy: An overview. *Theory into Practice, 41*(4), 212–218.

11. Dolan, T., Christens, B. D., & Lin, C. (2015). Combining youth organization and youth participatory action research to strengthen student voice in education reform. *Teachers College Record, 117*(13), 153–170.

12. Radd, S. I., Generett, G. G., Gooden, M. A., & Theoharis, G. (2021). *Five practices for equity-focused school leadership.* ASCD.

13. Lam, K. D. (2015). Teaching for liberation: Critical reflections in teacher education. *Multicultural Perspectives, 17*(3), 157–162.

14. Gay, G. (2018). *Culturally responsive teaching: Theory, research, and practice* (2nd ed.). Teachers College Press.

15. Valentine, J. (2009). *The instructional practices inventory: Using a student learning assessment to foster organizational learning.* National Staff Development Council, Annual Convention, St. Louis, MO.

Chapter 7

Establishing a Plan of Action When Instruction Is Not Inclusive

If we are truly invested in the improvement of teachers, and if we can accept that discrimination doesn't just live within individuals but is replicated, reinforced, and reified throughout social systems and constructs such as public education, then we must think about ways we can support teachers, over time, to improve their teaching when it is observed to be culturally damaging or culturally destructive. This does not mean we should give teachers a pass when they inflict harm on a group of students—quite the opposite. That said, culturally responsive instructional supervision requires feedback to help teachers understand, reflect, and improve their pedagogy.

Knowing how to balance holding teachers accountable for their instructional practices and ensuring that all students' cultural backgrounds and identities are valued and honored in the classroom is no easy task. It requires that, as educators, we move past the destructive notions of traditional Western education that assume one way of knowing and being and that values certain identities while further marginalizing others. To deconstruct and transform the instructional practices and traditions of US public schools in the way mentioned above, educators need to continually be aware of how their instruction is perceived and to reflect on how they learn to question assumptions about inclusion.

So how do instructional supervisors engage with teachers meaningfully if they have concerns about a lesson they just observed? What does this feedback look like, and how is it provided in a way that fosters formative growth and does not signal or actualize failure on a summative level? Who is ultimately responsible for supporting teachers in this type of reflection, and why is this critical in the effort to improve equitable outcomes in the US education system? When can these reflective points of feedback take place on the individual level, and where can these conversations on a group level help teachers improve in their pedagogical practices?

Some of the answers to these questions can be found in simply having clear guidelines and look-fors regarding what we see in the classroom. Essentially, what we measure is what we value, and if instructional supervisors are to make US society more equitable through educational practices, it must come from continually improving how we provide feedback about the kind of teaching that is observed daily in US classrooms. However, much of this work can be accomplished through traditional supervision practices that honor conversations, relationships, and time to reflect and improve, empowering teachers to drive their own reflection and learning.

One of the hardest and most challenging experiences any instructional supervisor will engage in is addressing instruction deemed unacceptable or harmful to students. It is a nuanced form of feedback that requires principals and instructional leaders to engage in ongoing conversations and documentation, if necessary, to help teachers understand how and what they are teaching must change and why. However, with the right approach, the kind of instructional supervision provided can help teachers move past culturally damaging or destructive practices with data about areas of improvement and conversations to support reflection and development.

DEFINING WHAT TEACHING LOOKS LIKE
THAT LACKS CULTURAL RESPONSIVENESS

Some of the tools and suggestions to determine what culturally responsive instructional supervision can look like were provided in chapter 6. It is crucial for principals and teacher leaders to define what culturally responsive instruction looks like, *as well as* what instruction looks like that lacks cultural responsiveness. While this can and should evolve over time based on the evolution of culturally responsive teaching within individual school buildings, there are look-fors educators can identify when instruction isn't culturally responsive.

Broadly speaking, this means ensuring observations look for instruction that values strong pedagogy, ensures an inclusive learning community, and centers emancipatory and liberating instruction. To ensure quality and equitable instruction is occurring throughout the schoolhouse, principals and teacher leaders that help form their representative instructional supervision teams must have the tools and the language to provide feedback about instruction that is not culturally responsive.

Instructional supervisors must be willing to disrupt, interrupt, and dismantle instructional practices that harm students and the communities they are intended to serve. Through this, instructional supervisors can begin to identify instruction that is exclusive in nature and develop a plan to help increase culturally responsive instruction in classrooms with individual support structures and building-wide improvement efforts.

Disrupting Deficit-Based Instruction That Promotes One Way of Knowing

Perhaps one of the most important roles for educational leaders to consider when engaging in culturally responsive instructional supervision is to disrupt the idea that there is one way of knowing, one way of understanding, and one way of showing comprehension or learning. Deficit-based instructional practices that reinforce lower-order thinking, worksheet-based repetition, and devalue student questions are all clear examples of instruction that prevent culturally responsive pedagogy. As such, it is critical to identify instructional approaches that lack asset-based approaches and to communicate with teachers about why this learning is problematic and inequitable via deficit-based instructional practices.

Interrupting Learning That Lacks Individual Connection

Another responsibility of providing culturally responsive instructional supervision is for principals and teacher leaders to interrupt learning that provides little opportunity for student voice or individual comprehension based on lived experiences. Instruction that fails to center student voice, lacks individualized support structures, and decontextualizes learning are all examples of pedagogy that lack cultural responsiveness. Identifying these instructional approaches and interrupting them requires that instructional leaders engage in discussions with teachers about how to increase student voice, representation, and connection to personalized lived experiences.

Dismantling Instruction That Centers Privileged Sociocultural Identities

When an instructional supervisor observes teaching that centers privileged sociocultural identities, it is their responsibility to dismantle these corresponding instructional practices that reinforce contextless learning, lack sociocultural awareness, and fail to address the marginalized experiences of various groups of people throughout the United States. Thus, to decenter privileged sociocultural identities, instructional supervisors must be willing to empower teachers to enact change, allow students to deeply reflect on the lived experiences of the marginalized, minoritized, and otherized in the United States and increase student representation and community identities.

DETERMINING FEEDBACK AND
SUPPORT STRUCTURES TO ADDRESS
PROBLEMATIC PEDAGOGIES

Part of the work of addressing problematic pedagogies is being able to reflect individually as well as engage in conversations in group settings to address what kind of instruction is occurring within a given educational system or context. This means that instructional supervisors must be able to lead and facilitate conversations about observed instruction and, using data points, engage in reflective conversations about how to shift instructional practices to be more culturally responsive. Engaging in this work takes time, requires continually (un)learning, and demands a relentless commitment to ensuring all students feel like they belong in the schoolhouse and can receive a rigorous education.

Supporting ongoing growth and development of instructional practices can and should be addressed in various ways, as noted in figure 7.1. While this will be covered in detail in part III, instructional growth and development always starts with the self (chapter 8), is expanded by reflecting with critical

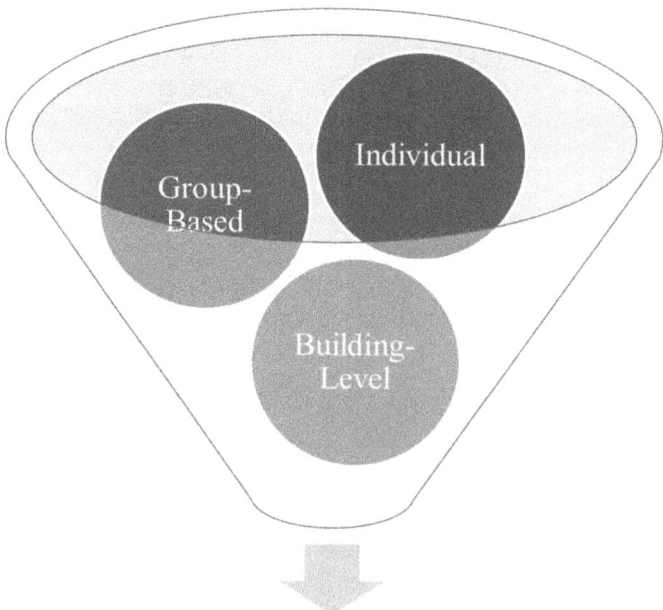

Development of Culturally
Responsive Supervision Structures

Figure 7.1. Supervisory Support Structures for Culturally Responsive Outcomes

colleagues in small groups or departments/grade-level teams (chapter 9), and is codified at the building level with peer-led observations and ongoing conversations about data in large faculty settings (chapter 10). A majority (we estimate roughly 75 to 85 percent of educators) will engage in what is right for students and ensure there are equitable outcomes for learning.

But what happens when there is an individual issue that needs more attention than can be addressed with the structures listed above? What happens when an individual teacher needs more time, attention, formative feedback, and support to increase their reflection to develop culturally responsive instructional practices? How can instructional supervisors meet an educator where they are, developmentally, and give them what they need to improve their instructional practices? How can leaders engage teachers to connect with the identities of their students to make learning relevant, and how can they reflect on their own positionality to inform teaching?

Part of this work can come in the form of a member of the representative supervision team peeling off from the building-wide data collection process and focusing on the individual development of a teacher who needs more intense support structures. By targeting ongoing data collection of classroom observations with an individual teacher, the representative supervision team can increase the amount of data available about an individual teacher. The idea is that with increased data that is collected over a couple of weeks, there should be a sufficient small dataset of 20 to 30 observation data points that help the teacher measure and reflect on what someone else has observed.

Thus, over the course of a quarter or a semester, a teacher who has been observed to have problematic pedagogical practices can use formative and ongoing observational data to empower themselves to include and identify culturally responsive teaching practices that can be shown to have changed over time. With individual input, a teacher like this can work collaboratively with a trusted colleague of their choosing (or selected by the supervision team if necessary) to help drive reflection and ongoing development about instruction. From there, individualized professional development opportunities can be targeted, implemented, and reflect upon. The cycle then continues.

This level of intervention can also include a member of the representative supervision team modeling an instructional approach, which is common in professional development schools and practiced in other parts of the world like Japan and Finland.[1] Additionally, individual teachers who are struggling with problematic pedagogical practices should engage with literature or social media that can help inform culturally responsive instructional practices. These can be led by the teacher but might need the assistance of a member of the supervision team to help start this learning process.

Ultimately, the goal of more individualized support is to see growth in cultural proficiency in the physical classroom, student engagement and interactions, and empowering students to address inequities they see and experience in their everyday lives. This means that a teacher can move through the cultural proficiency continuum[2] where they increasingly become culturally competent in advocating for equity for all students the school serves (see figure 7.2). As such, an instructional supervisor might also need to support a developing teacher by creating lesson plans that incorporate greater student representation and diverse sociocultural identities.

However, part of addressing problematic pedagogies is also rooted in the ability of an instructional supervisor to identify and confront conflict. This means that principals and teacher leaders alike must be willing to address concerns based on objective observations and with an approach that can help build culturally responsive practices based on relational trust. None of this work is about blaming individuals for prejudiced or biased beliefs, but rather it is about deconstructing a system that has helped reinforce deficit-based mindsets and the elimination of cultures that aren't privileged in US schools and society. This work requires patience, focus, and love.

With that said, this practice also requires valuing growth, development, reflection, and improvement over time. While it might seem counterintuitive, culturally responsive instructional supervision is an approach to school improvement that doesn't see someone as a failure if they engage in teaching that lacks cultural responsiveness but rather as a teaching moment and learning opportunity.

With the right feedback, and with feedback that is continuous and ongoing, we estimate that 90 to 95 percent of teachers, over time, will be able to show growth in their cultural competence and how this translates into instruction practices. How instructional supervisors differentiate their feedback is critical in ensuring instructional improvement is delivered to meet the developmental needs of all teachers—and their students.

Figure 7.2. Supervisory Steps within the Cultural Proficiency Continuum

FURTHER DEVELOPING REFLECTIVE
AND INCLUSIVE INSTRUCTION

Given the various abilities of teachers based on their experience, expertise, and personal ability to reflect and grow over time, principals and teacher leaders need to consider how developmental supervision[3] can be applied to formative feedback structures that lead to improvements in culturally responsive teaching practices. While the developmental framework has been applied in various ways throughout supervision literature, it is just beginning to be reflected in ways that address inequitable instruction.[4]

Instructional supervisors must be able to determine how to differentiate between directive control, directive informational, collaborative, and nondirective forms of feedback that are best suited to the needs of teachers. Figure 7.3 highlights how supervisors can determine how to apply developmental supervision through the lens of cultural proficiency. This requires instructional leaders to interpret and decide the best path forward to develop cultural competence within individual educators.

At the heart of this work is the ability of an instructional supervisor to apply nuanced feedback about instruction based on their own understanding of cultural proficiency, interpersonal relationship skills, and the observed and communicated aptitude of a teacher to reflect upon, develop, and improve their instructional practices. Having a developmental approach to providing culturally responsive instructional supervision can help principals and teacher leaders determine next steps in the feedback process. The following section provides detailed examples of each approach.

Directive Control Approach for Culturally Responsive Instructional Supervision

While it hopefully does not need to occur often, sometimes an instructional supervisor will need to directly assign ways to improve instruction that is

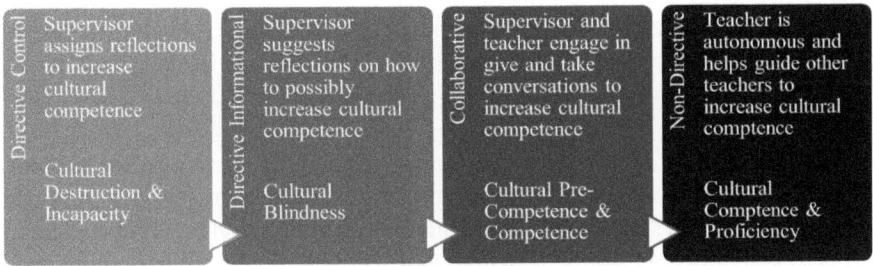

Figure 7.3.   Developmental Supervision Applying a Cultural Proficiency Lens

observed to be culturally destructive or stereotyping cultures. An example of this is if an observation occurs where a culture, race, or ethnicity is mocked, erased, trivialized, or appropriated as a central aspect of the instruction (e.g., dressing up as Native Americans at Thanksgiving, celebrating Christmas within the curriculum, etc.).

When this occurs, principals and teacher leaders must use opportunities such as this to increase cultural capacity and competence by directly assigning methods of reflecting on how and in what ways this type of instruction continues to minoritize, marginalize, and otherize students. As noted by Khalifa,[5] "educational leaders and teachers will either reproduce oppression, or they will contest it" (p. 19).

This type of feedback helps establish the response moving forward regarding how a teacher might improve their own cultural competence and begin to mend relationships with students and families they might have damaged. The key here is less about making someone feel bad about the transgression and more about how to model reflecting on why the instruction was culturally damaging and how to be more aware of future approaches to instruction and student engagement. The assigned feedback can include a teacher reading a practitioner-friendly article, watching a video, engaging on various social media platforms, or joining a book study. However, the growth comes from the ensuing conversations and self-reflection.

Once an instructional supervisor has engaged in the directive control approach to support the development of culturally responsive teaching, they must then also model how to talk about and reflect upon what was assigned to promote growth and development. In these follow-up conversations, principals and instructional leaders must share their own thoughts on the assigned material, model vulnerability by detailing their own growth to unlearn culturally damaging and deficit-oriented perceptions they learn through socialization, and ensure the teacher that they are capable of developing their own equity mindset.

It is a process that requires patience and, at times, might very well feel overwhelming and hopeless to the instructional supervisor themself. It would also be foolish to think this work is easy or straightforward. Principals and teacher leaders engaged in this work must be cognizant of their own fatigue around equity implementation, especially how this influences their physiological responses and the stressors this work can have on mental and emotional health.

If, as an instructional supervisor, you are physically stimulated or mentally tired, providing feedback at that time might be unwise; we advise you to wait until you are physically and emotionally calm to provide feedback about what exactly was culturally destructive or inappropriate within the context of observational data. Over time, however, we believe instructional supervisors can develop a rapport with teachers who struggle with implementing culturally responsive teaching practices and eventually be able to shift toward the next developmental step in the process of suggesting how to improve.

Directive Informational Approach for Culturally Responsive Instructional Supervision

When a teacher engages in instruction that suggests there is no discrimination in US society or they fail to acknowledge privileged sociocultural identities, an instructional supervisor can help the teacher continue to increase their cultural competence. An example of this might come from an observation where the teacher verbalizes how race, ethnicity, and gender don't play a role in the modern United States (e.g., teaching about the history of the Thirteenth Amendment and Nineteenth Amendment but then saying they are not needed today). If (and when) this occurs, instructional supervisors can suggest how to improve culturally responsive teaching practices.

In this approach, a principal and/or teacher leader makes recommendations and provides ideas on how a teacher can acknowledge the various sociocultural identities that exist in their classroom. With this approach, the instructional supervisor is directing the teacher to information the teacher knows exists but perhaps doesn't want to acknowledge, namely, the need to move away from concepts such as meritocracy and to recognize that inequities are present in our society and thus require educators to acknowledge these inequities.

This type of feedback is considered a strong nudge or warm demander and, again, requires the instructional supervisor to follow up to engage in a conversation about the suggested reflection and intervention or to understand how the teacher reflected on their own. Applying directive informational feedback to support culturally responsive teaching should be seen as a bridge intervention to help a teacher eventually engage in a collaborative discussion about becoming more culturally competent.

When following up with a teacher to engage in the suggested reflection, principals and instructional leaders should focus on conversations that acknowledge how students are marginalized, minoritized, and otherized and address their own experiences in learning to recognize the different lived experiences of groups within the United States. In this developmental approach, the goal for instructional supervisors is to help the teacher learn how to engage in conversations about instruction that acknowledges the need for inclusion and representation.

When applying the directive informational approach, principals and teacher leaders must learn to serve as a light that illuminates the inequities often perpetuated by the US PK–12 public school system. While instructional supervisors might be frustrated with cultural blindness displayed by teachers, modeling how to improve culturally responsive teaching through suggestions is the next step in helping teachers develop their own growth at the individual level. Each time feedback is provided that is suggested and informational, a teacher is learning how to engage in this reflective work on their own and is more capable of becoming culturally competent.

Collaborative Approach for Culturally Responsive Instructional Supervision

The goal of principals and teacher leaders engaging in culturally responsive instructional supervision is to help teachers participate in collaborative conversations about their instructional practices. In this developmental phase, teachers might fluctuate between cultural precompetence and cultural competence, but by and large they are leading their own reflective conversations with others. Examples of this can occur through observations that acknowledge privileged sociocultural identities, but sometimes occur in limited or prescribed ways (e.g., lessons on LGBTQIA+ leaders only during Pride month or ensuring representation of race but only in Language Arts, etc.).

These moments provide an opportunity for instructional supervisors to engage in conversations about instruction that value inclusion and belonging *in every instructional setting* and throughout the school year—not just limited to certain spaces or times. Perhaps the most important component of this type of feedback is to highlight, celebrate, and uphold observed instruction that is culturally competent (or precompetent) to make sure it is positively reinforced and occurs again. The conversations that can occur during this developmental approach are about supporting development of teachers' consciousness. Subsequently, this approach develops the culture of the building.

Using the collaborative approach to support the development of culturally responsive teaching requires an instructional supervisor to distinguish between cultural precompetence and cultural competence. By engaging in collaborative conversations, principals and teacher leaders can assess if the culturally responsive instruction is occurring but in limited ways (precompetence), or if it is occurring in a way that values sociocultural differences and is used to educate students about gross societal inequities. Instructional supervisors should celebrate the observed equitable instruction and ask how it might be applied throughout the school.

As principals and teacher leaders engage in this developmental approach, it is important to remember that the goal of culturally responsive teaching is to empower students not just to understand the inequities in US society, but to deconstruct these inequities and empower teachers and students to enact change. In doing so, instructional supervisors should support teachers by collaborating about how they might develop lesson plans that create a more socially just democracy and to better support the community the school serves. The goal, ultimately, is to help encourage teachers who are culturally proficient and autonomous in cultural responsiveness development.

Nondirective Approach for Culturally Responsive Instructional Supervision

Based on developmental needs and observed expertise engaging in culturally responsive pedagogy, supervisors of instruction may decide to take a nondirective approach when considering what is best for a teacher and what is needed to support their instructional practices. This should only be used when teachers have consistently shown cultural competence or cultural proficiency in developing their reflective stance about their own teaching. This occurs when instructional leaders use and apply a culturally responsive instructional supervision lens *and* they observe teaching that calls out inequities through instruction and with curricular materials.

Supervisors should also decide when to use a nondirective approach with a teacher when they see instruction and teacher leadership that openly advocates for making learning experiences equitable and inclusive for all children. In this situation, supervisors should see these teacher leaders as part of a formal or informal teacher leadership team that is capable of influencing others to become culturally competent or culturally proficient. At this developmental stage, conversations that take place between instructional supervisors and teachers should focus on distributing leadership among teams, departments, and other organizational structures.

At its core, using the nondirective approach as a culturally responsive instructional supervisor requires ongoing observations that a teacher has an unwavering belief that, through an equitable education system, the United States can create a more inclusive democracy that serves all students. To do so requires ongoing and continual reflection about the privileged sociocultural identities of the teacher the supervisor is supporting, but also observing how the teacher considers the experiences of marginalized students in their classroom. Observing teaching and leadership that addresses the marginalized experiences of students should be the precursor to this approach.

Unfortunately, the likelihood of eventually using a nondirective approach with every teacher isn't reasonable or plausible. To ensure that education systems do not discriminate and do not perpetuate inequities requires instructional leaders to acknowledge the decades and maybe even centuries of work that will be required to deconstruct and recreate a more equitable school system that teaches students about the discriminatory foundation of US society *and* empowers them to enact change within US society. Over time, and with the right support structures, instructional supervisors can help support a more critical understanding of pedagogy.

SEEING CRITICALITY AS A TOOL
FOR EMANCIPATION

As described by Freire,[6] we can support the development of a critical consciousness within teachers as a tool to understand the historical and social realities of our world and our society. Critical consciousness is at the heart of culturally responsive instructional supervision regarding the mindset that is needed for instructional leaders to address historical and societal inequities within the United States. Then, over time, principals and teacher leaders help other educators in the building develop a clear understanding of how schools function as oppressive systems and help students engage in the lived experience of those who are marginalized.[7]

The development of critical consciousness is a powerful learning environment where teachers and students learn together and address sociopolitical inequities that are rampant throughout US society. Through liberatory educational opportunities and experiences, principals and teacher leaders can engage in the praxis of culturally responsive instructional supervision to reach new understandings and awareness about the discriminatory realities of US society. Through this work, educators can raise their consciousness about the meaning of education—something many teachers struggle with currently.[8]

Throughout all content areas and subjects, students can and should engage in issues of social justice and finds ways to collaborate on addressing social inequities through the exploration and application of content knowledge. This includes the need for classroom learning to value social responsibility, human dignity, and economic equality, which should all be present and centered in a democratic society. Deeply connected with this work is the need to focus on the social-emotional well-being of students, which has historically been ignored through the failed accountability experiment and should be a core and foundational component of increasing consciousness.

At the most basic approach, the goal of providing this kind of formative feedback is to use culturally responsive instructional supervision to drive learning among students and for teachers to continually question assumptions about the intent of education in the United States and the kind of self-awareness that is needed to engage in learning about political, social, and economic realities.[9] Through a developmental supervision approach that applies a cultural proficiency lens, instructional leaders can help teachers and students engage in their own critical consciousness. In doing so, a school will be more likely to be able to serve the needs of its local community.

DEVELOPING THE SCAFFOLDING
FOR TRANSFORMATION

The prior three chapters address how supervision can no longer be a one- or two-person act—that if the education system is to achieve equitable outcomes, it must increase representation in how feedback about instruction is provided. Additionally, with ongoing data collection, teams of teachers can reflect on observed, objective data and make plans to access professional development to increase the ability to provide culturally responsive teaching. With that as the foundation, instructional supervisors can begin the process of providing individualized, developmentally appropriate feedback to help increase critical consciousness in teachers.

The upcoming three chapters will provide a framework for how principals and teacher leaders can scaffold the development of culturally responsive teachers who can evolve within a CCRI. With ongoing and formative feedback, instructional supervisors can ensure growth occurs (1) at the individual level, (2) among peers through critical colleagues, and (3) through the development of expertise among faculty through peer-led observations. Through this work, the intent of culturally responsive instructional supervision is to value growth through various intrapersonal and interpersonal reflections.

To support reflective stances about instruction that value culturally responsive teaching requires instructional leaders to lead in a way that most practitioners might avoid or resist. The work will be fraught with struggles, disagreements, and public debates about what school *is for* and whom it is *intended* to serve; historically, that has been those with privileged sociocultural identities. Schools can and should still serve these students—but not at the demise and struggle of those who have been marginalized, minoritized, and otherized in US schools and society. It is that challenge that requires a complete paradigm shift in how educators think about instructional outcomes.

NOTES

1. Lutton, L. (2012). Japanese strategy for improving teachers is catching on in Chicago. *The Hechinger Report.* https://hechingerreport.org/japanese-strategy-for-improving-teachers-is-catching-on-in-chicago/

2. Lindsey, R. B., Robins, K. N., & Terrell, R. D. (2009). *Cultural proficiency: A manual for school leaders.* Corwin.

3. Glickman, C. D., Gordon, S. P., & Ross-Gordon, J. M. (2018). *Supervision and instructional leadership: A developmental approach* (10th ed.). Pearson.

4. Virella, P. (forthcoming). Applying the supervisory behavior continuum to determine a plan of action and support when teaching isn't culturally responsive. In I. M.

Mette, D. R. Cormier, & Y. Oliveras-Ortiz (Eds.), *Culturally responsive instructional supervision: Instructional leadership for equitable and emancipatory outcomes.* Teachers College Press.

5. Khalifa, M. (2020). *Culturally responsive school leadership* (4th ed.). Harvard Education Press.

6. Freire, P. (1970). *Pedagogy of the oppressed.* Seabury Press.

7. Waite, S. R. (2021). Towards a theory of critical consciousness: A new direction for the development of instructional and supervisory leaders. *Journal of Educational Supervision, 4*(2), 65–79. https://doi.org/10.31045/jes.4.2.4

8. Waite, S. R. (forthcoming). The criticality of consciousness in professional development. In I. M. Mette, D. R. Cormier, & Y. Oliveras-Ortiz (Eds.), *Culturally responsive instructional supervision: Instructional leadership for equitable and emancipatory outcomes.* Teachers College Press.

9. Ladson–Billings, G. (1998). Just what is critical race theory and what's it doing in a nice field like education? *Qualitative Studies in Education, 11*(1), 7–24; Ladson–Billings, G. (1999). Preparing teachers for diverse student populations: A critical race theory perspective. *Review of Research in Education, 24*, 211–247; Ladson–Billings, G. (1999). Preparing teachers for diverse student populations: A critical race theory perspective. *Review of Research in Education, 24*, 211–247.

PART III

Supporting Ongoing Growth and Development of Culturally Responsive Instruction

Chapter 8

Growth Starts with the Self

The road to becoming a more culturally responsive teacher won't happen in isolation—and it won't occur overnight. It requires ongoing feedback that is formative and supportive and gives people the psychological and emotional safety (i.e., grace) to try and fail. Learning how to make education more equitable is ongoing and will take a lifetime for the current generation of educators. As such, the process of creating an equitable US society will be slow and methodical,[1] one that requires educators to be more organized and advocate more passionately than those that wish to see more discriminatory outcomes that have privileged some people over others, including but not limited to identities such as race, gender, and class.

However, through culturally responsive instructional supervision, there is great possibility to help drive change in instruction on an individual level, which can then drive change in smaller groups, which can then be transferred to teams or departments, which can then influence an entire building. With developmental feedback based on the cultural proficiency of individual teachers, as well as through objective observed data from classroom walkthroughs, growth among educators is possible. To begin this transformation requires that teachers accept that growth must start within the self—often a process that can be scary and even seem impossible to many educators.

Yet individual growth about how to make education a more equitable system doesn't have to be the boogeyman many moderates and conservatives make it out to be. Every teacher has a reason they entered the profession, and given the pressures of accountability and the renewed attention to ensuring social justice occurs within the United States after Black Lives Matter and the public killing of George Floyd, most would likely admit they *know* there are gross inequities in US society but they *do not know* how to address these issues given the accountability demands of their job.[2] And that is exactly what culturally responsive instructional supervision can help address.

USING AGENCY TO ADDRESS THE
PURPOSE OF EDUCATION

Gay's definition of culturally responsive teaching[3] focuses explicitly on rigor and student outcomes, specifically that students will achieve at higher levels when they are provided learning opportunities aligned with their own cultural identities and lived experiences (i.e., sociocultural construction). As such, education cannot be expected to contribute to a pluralistic society where *all* students experience equity and excellence if education does not address how history and culture influence academic outcomes. To accomplish these goals, our education system must help students understand how to relate to one another to help develop a more inclusive US society.

At the core of this movement is the ability for teachers to acknowledge that high achievement for all students (not just some) is not only possible, but also necessary for the long-term health of US society, democracy, and citizenship.[4] As an education system, we can and should expect students to achieve at high levels, but it must be done through instruction that considers the identities and lived experiences of all students—especially those minoritized, marginalized, and otherized—not in the name of federal or state accountability systems. The purpose of education, then, becomes one that focuses on rigor and achievement in the name of acknowledging our brutal and violent racialized past—and how this plays out in present-day US society.

Instructional supervisors can support the beginning of the journey for personal self-growth by asking the question, "What is the purpose of education?" Many educators enter the profession for idealistic reasons; however, over the course of a few years or partially through a career, many practitioners become disillusioned and find their experience as a teacher is not what they envisioned and hoped for.[5] Yet this is exactly why this question needs to be asked, and it is also why culturally responsive instructional supervisors should support the asking and answering of this question.

From this reflection, a whole domino of answers and likely more questions, as well as general comments, can arise. These might include but are not limited to some of the following:

- Do I have the ability to impact meaningful change for the marginalized students I serve?
- Do I have the capacity to impact meaningful change for the marginalized students I serve?
- Do I have the energy to engage in the work of culturally responsive instructional leadership and teaching, given that I am already struggling

to manage my current workload and the additional mental load of differentiating based on identity?

- Have I prepared myself to address potential objections and protests from parents if I choose to address historically controversial issues such as racism, homophobia, or xenophobia in my teaching?
- Have I reconciled my beliefs and contradictions in the importance of this work with my reluctance to influence my peers and the potential tension that may arise as a result? Can I engage in this work while maintaining a positive relationship with my colleagues?
- Have I taken the necessary steps to balance my commitment to being culturally proficient in my teaching with the legal requirements mandated by the state? Have I sought or advocated for resources or support systems to help me navigate this challenge?

These problem-posing questions are not invalid—but they are also not a reason to continue with the status quo perpetuated and reinforced by the current US education system. Each person has the agency to become more loving, more inclusive, and more reflective. And culturally responsive instructional supervisors must help teachers ask and answer these very tough and problematizing questions.

Unequivocally, teachers must be provided with formative feedback that enables them to understand that they can provide meaningful instruction that helps historically marginalized students see themselves more in the curriculum and feel empowered to address inequities through instruction. Teachers must be provided with instructional supervision that centers diversity and identity, not considers it an afterthought, because this type of focus will help drive increased student achievement rather than harm it.[6] Critical to the work is the need for instructional leaders, principals, and teacher leaders alike to protect equity-minded instruction from public scrutiny.

Teachers also need support from instructional supervisors to understand that instruction in the schoolhouse can no longer be protected behind closed doors. Deprivatizing instruction not only ensures all students have access to inclusive instruction that allows them to feel like they belong, but it also is connected to the idea of a CCRI where the strength of a group of educators is far more powerful than a singular teacher.

Most important, all of this can be done by meeting the legal requirements of each state. Either by teaching directly to standards that are aligned to the sociocultural identities of students or by providing countless opportunities for students to examine, reflect on, and comment about their observations regarding statistics, history, and literature that proves the ongoing inequities within US society, teachers can provide opportunities to empower students to identify and deconstruct the inequities that are lived experiences and/or that they so readily see.

OWNING CONTENT EXPERTISE

To enhance their ability to implement culturally responsive teaching, teachers should engage in self-reflection and develop a strong belief in their expertise in the cultural context of their students. With these skills, teachers can tailor their instructional approaches to incorporate their students' sociocultural identities and lived experiences. This is no different than approaching the instructional needs of a student who has modifications or accommodations to support their learning. The goal of instruction is not to create one way of teaching and learning, but to connect students with learning opportunities and to understand the assets each student brings into the school and classroom.[7] Teachers can accomplish this by connecting their expertise to their students' sociocultural identities and needs.

While not definitive or exhaustive, the following examples show how instructional supervisors can provide individual feedback and support to teachers individually in implementing culturally responsive instructional practices in their classrooms. To be clear, not everything can be viewed through a culturally responsive lens, but a lot can be based on the ability of a teacher to be creative and apply content expertise in a way that speaks to the identities and the lived experience of each child. Below are some examples of approaches teachers *might* take to improving outcomes for their students.

Math

- If the learning objective is to compare means and determine if two groups are statistically significantly different, a math teacher can provide various real-world datasets about social outcomes for various groups across the United States. These data might include outcomes such as life expectancy, the average number of times individuals are arrested or incarcerated over the course of a lifetime, and access to advanced coursework in PK–12 education systems. Using content expertise, the teacher can help guide students to determine if there are statistically significant differences between groups and ask students to make inferences as to why this occurs.
- If the learning objective requires students to understand and differentiate between linear, exponential, and quadratic equations and patterns, a math teacher can provide real-world examples about each of those functions. These examples might include a basketball being shot or a football

being thrown (quadratic), the rate of infection for yearly flu or COVID infections (exponential), or budgeting for new clothes or the amount of time it takes to travel from one place to another (linear). Based on the identities of children in their classroom, teachers can apply their content expertise to unpack other patterns they see in their day-to-day lives.

- If the learning objective is to use computation and estimation based on patterns, a math teacher can provide students with a variety of real-world examples that exist in local areas, within the state they live, or across the United States. These might include average income as it varies across education level, racial/ethnic percentages based on school district zones or zip codes, or school funding discrepancies across spatial locations. Leveraging their content expertise, teachers can help students describe the patterns they see and empower them to make inferences about what these mean for social equality.

Language Arts

- If the learning objective is to form predictions about what will happen next in a story, a language arts teacher can provide excerpts that students can choose from, including but not limited to environmental shifts, different lived experiences of diaspora communities as they migrate, or various childhood experiences growing up in urban or rural places. Using their content expertise, a language arts teacher can support students in their writing development and encourage them to provide examples from their own experiences as to why they made the predictions they did about what will happen next in the story. Students can then have the option to share these across the classroom to have a better understanding of how they might relate to one another and to learn from each other about different lived experiences.
- If the learning objective requires students to use symbolism in short stories, a language arts teacher can provide examples of published materials and ask students to analyze the various messages about society portrayed through the stories. These published materials might include topics such as the pressure from family dynamics, the value of women in US society, the need for hope in a brutal economic system, or the role of race in US society. Based on various identities and lived experiences of students in their classroom, teachers can use their expertise in their content area to help students understand the role of symbolism in literature and how interpretation might vary from student to student.
- If the learning objective is to create a three-paragraph constructed response that advocates for a position, a language arts teacher can allow students to pick a position that applies to their everyday life. The teacher

might need to provide examples, which could include the benefits of more recess time for physical health, concerns about a community's access to clean drinking water, or how drug use disorder impacts community members. Using their content expertise, teachers can help students feel empowered to advocate for themselves.

Social Studies

- If the learning objective is to identify how US policies in the eighteenth and nineteenth centuries influenced relations with Native American nations, a social studies teacher can support students to engage in document analysis of archived materials detailing signed treaties and comparing this with land acquisition as well as the Monroe Doctrine. These activities might detail the relationships with various Native American tribes during the eighteenth and nineteenth centuries, but students could also analyze how this has impacted tribal relationships and the development of Native American nations in present-day US policies. Using their content expertise, a social studies teacher can guide students to make their own inferences about US policies.
- If the learning objective requires students to understand civil disobedience in US history, a social studies teacher can provide a variety of real-world examples that students can choose from, including the various roles in the fight for women's suffrage; the influence of Martin Luther King Jr., Malcolm X, Fred Hampton, Fannie Lou Hamer, and others in the civil rights movement; Muhammad Ali and others who burned draft cards in protest of the Vietnam War; and the various roles people played in the Gay Activist Alliance movement of the 1970s. Based on individual interests of students, social studies teachers can use their content expertise to support students and deepen their understanding of these movements on US history.
- If the learning objective is to understand the election process in the United States, a social studies teacher can provide various examples of transitions of power throughout US history. These might include an overview of the Presidential Transition Act of 1963 to ensure peaceful transition of power, how seven states seceded when Lincoln won the presidency, the recount when President Bush ultimately won over Al Gore, and the insurrection that occurred on January 6, 2021, when President Trump claimed widespread fraud. Using content expertise, teachers can help detail the importance of democratic transitions.

Science

- If the learning objective is to use the scientific method, a science teacher can support students to engage in social behavior studies that include observations about human behavior. The variables that could be used in the scientific method might include basic demographic variables that the students can pick for themselves, including gender, race, and other sociocultural identities of their choice. Using their content expertise, a science teacher can help students create a study that allows them to collect and analyze data about human behavior, including observations and reflections that detail implicit bias within a social setting.
- If the learning objective requires students to understand the water cycle, a science teacher can provide foundational instruction to the objective and extend the learning by asking students to consider how this applies to their everyday lives. Examples of extending this learning might include how the water cycle is magnified by climate change as well as what groups are disproportionately impacted based on geography and spatial concentrations of people. Based on the identities and interests of students, teachers can apply their expertise to help students look for and identify other impacts the water cycle has on society more broadly.
- If the learning objective is to understand the importance of biological discoveries in the twentieth century, a science teacher can provide students with a variety of real-world examples of studies that led to institutional review boards, such as the Tuskegee Study, experiments conducted by the Nazis, and the cells stolen from Henrietta Lacks for the cloning of cells. Leveraging their expertise in their content, science teachers can help students understand the importance of ethics in biological experiments and discoveries and support students making connections about biological discoveries in modern US society, including concerns of genetic mapping and the cloning of animals and body parts.

Educators who are defined as elementary teachers, as well as those who are defined as elective teachers (i.e., art, music, industrial technology, physical education, computer programming, etc.), will need to determine the developmentally appropriate implementation of culturally responsive teaching that enables students to see themselves in the curriculum and does not privilege certain sociocultural identities over others. However, the outline above provides a decent starting point for how all teachers can ensure they apply their content expertise in a way that connects to individual students in their classrooms.

Regardless of content, all teachers do have the agency to make their classrooms more equitable. This can be observed through a variety of curricular materials that ensure representation of what is being learned reflects the population of a classroom *as well as* the US population. As such, it is critical for teachers to leverage their content expertise in a way that focuses on rigorous instruction and is done in the name of making the United States a more democratic and inclusive society. It is critical for principals and teacher leaders who engage in culturally responsive instructional supervision to help support the growth of teachers on a personal and professional level.

LEARNING TO ADDRESS THE NEEDS OF SOCIETY OVER OUR OWN COMFORT

For some teachers, and for some instructional supervisors for that matter, it will be difficult to evolve in a way that supports the formative and ongoing development of the instructional practices of educators that helps them see their own privileges. However, there can be much growth supporting culturally responsive instruction when educators accept and acknowledge how their own experiences have at times been marginalized in traditional US education systems. And once instructional leaders can help teachers see how education oppresses even those with some or many privileged identities, the schoolhouse can begin to be reimagined.

For many teachers, the education system is a comfortable, powerful, middle-class experience. The classroom affords safety, typically a lifetime appointment, and usually a moderately good retirement. It also gives most people a sense of *belonging* in the longest socialization process that occurs in modern society. By becoming a teacher, you are part of the system—and part of the work to becoming a culturally responsive instructor is to constantly remind yourself that societal systems in the United States produce inequitable outcomes for minoritized, marginalized, and otherized groups.[8]

For some educators it might be hard to talk about racial inequities—in fact for most White educators, it almost certainly will be. However, many people do know what marginalization feels like based on gender, or class, or orientation, or ability, or age, among others. And if you can understand one form of marginalization, chances are you can begin to understand others, even if it doesn't impact you directly.

By focusing on growth that starts with the self, educators can continually engage in a process of identifying what outcomes are inequitable, addressing how to plan for remediation of the inequities, and implementing the actions to address and eliminate the inequities. Figure 8.1 details the continual process of how instructional supervisors can eliminate instructional inequities in the schoolhouse through specific interventions. Once implementation

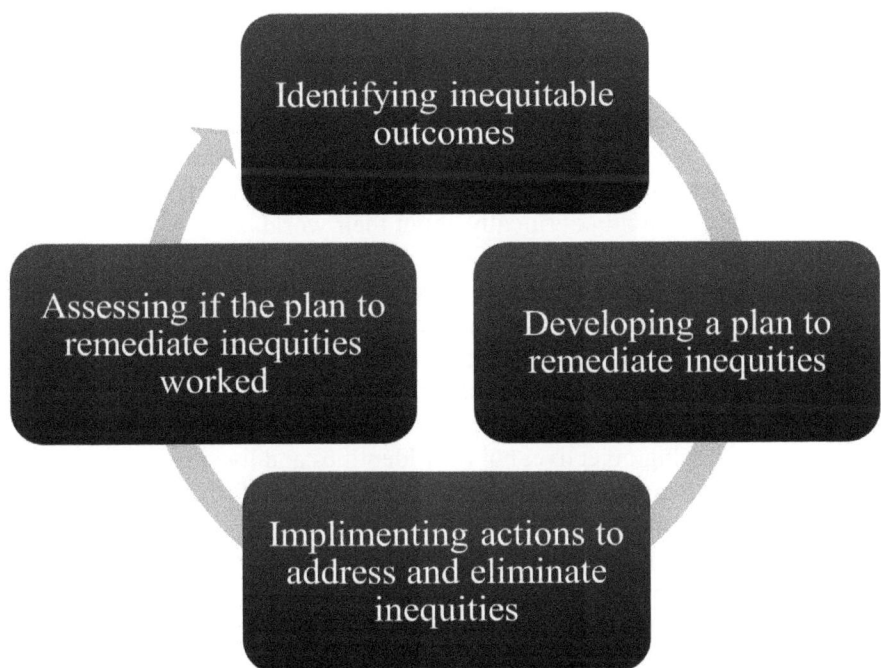

Figure 8.1. The Continual Process of Eliminating Instructional Inequities

has occurred, educators assess if the effort worked, after which the process repeats itself and continues indefinitely.

At the very center of culturally responsive instructional supervision is the core belief that, as educators, we must focus on the greater good of society and not ignore the needs of children or continue with a system just because it is hard to change what we were taught. To make a change on a system level, teachers, teacher leaders, and principals need to work collaboratively to support a school culture that values reflection, values ongoing feedback about instruction, and sees education as a vehicle to make our society more equitable and inclusive. Even if the work feels overwhelming, there are actions teachers can take every day to help make education liberatory.

KNOWING PEDAGOGICAL LOOK-FORS
WHEN REFLECTING ON TEACHING

Teachers can improve their practice by regularly reflecting on their teaching practice. Instructional leaders can guide this process by encouraging teachers to revisit chapter 6 and explore how they can utilize data to increase their self-awareness of the instructional practices and interactions used in their classroom. One way to assess equitable outcomes for all students is to consider the rigor of the pedagogical practices being provided to students. Consider if higher-order thinking is provided, how the knowledge is applied, and the level to which student questions are valued and addressed. Focusing on these aspects of instruction are important and are the foundation to empower students to think critically about their world.

Another way for teachers to reflect on their own teaching is the level to which they create a community of inclusive learning. This includes how and in what ways student voice plays a role in learning, particularly how voice and identity are honored as strengths that are brought to the classroom.[9] Culturally responsive instruction also considers how checking for comprehension to offer individualized support structures increases understanding of not only the learning objective, but how identities and lived experiences play a critical role in learning. This requires validating and affirming teaching that sees each student as an individual.

Perhaps the most important reflection a culturally responsive instructor can engage in is how and in what ways their instruction is emancipatory and liberating for students who are marginalized, minoritized, and otherized.[10] Teachers can and should reflect on how instruction empowers students to address inequities experienced at the local level, to center sociocultural identities at the center of the learning, and to value the physical space created that allows people from all visible and nonvisible identities to belong. In doing so, educators begin the process of transforming their classroom from a deficit-oriented perspective to one that values assets.

Learning how to grow intrapersonally—where teachers accept feedback about their instructional practices but then specifically engage in their own personal development that is ongoing and driven by reflections about the self—is crucial to the culturally responsive instructional supervision process. Systems may perpetuate inequities, but individuals can help create new systems, ones that value a sense of belonging and inclusion *if* people are willing to grow on their own. However, change cannot occur in isolation and requires development in small groups to help push learning and application in new and transformative ways.

NOTES

1. Willey, C., & Magee, P. A. (2019). Whiteness as a barrier to becoming a culturally relevant teacher: Clinical experiences and the role of supervision. *Journal of Educational Supervision, 1*(2), 33–51. https://doi.org/10.31045/jes.1.2.3

2. Milner, IV, H. R. (2020). *Start where you are, but don't stay there: Understanding diversity, opportunity gaps, and teaching in today's classrooms* (2nd ed.). Harvard Education Press.

3. Gay, G. (2018). *Culturally responsive teaching: Theory, research, and practice* (2nd ed.). Teachers College Press.

4. Glickman, C. D., & Mette, I. M. (2020). *The essential renewal of America's schools: A leadership guide for democratizing schools from the inside out.* Teachers College Press.

5. Oliveira, S., Roberto, M. S., Veiga-Simão, A. M., & Marques-Pinto, A. (2021). A meta-analysis of the impact of social and emotional learning interventions on teachers' burnout symptoms. *Educational Psychology Review, 33*(4), 1779–1808.

6. Villegas, A. M., & Lucas, T. (2007). The culturally responsive teacher. *Educational Leadership, 64*(6), 28–33.

7. López, F. A. (2017). Altering the trajectory of the self-fulfilling prophecy: Asset-based pedagogy and classroom dynamics. *Journal of Teacher Education, 68*(2), 193–212.

8. Cormier, D. R., & Pandey, T. (2021). Semiotic analysis of a foundational textbook used widely across educational supervision. *Journal of Educational Supervision, 4*(2), 101–132.

9. Muhammad, G. (2022). On identity. *Voices From the Middle, 30*(1), 14–16.

10. Love, B. L. (2019b). *We want to do more than survive: Abolitionist teaching and the pursuit of educational reform.* Beacon Press.

Chapter 9

Learning to Grow with Critical Colleagues

In the development of a CCRI, growth must first occur and take hold within the self. Individuals decide to grow when they are in charge of their own development, which is why culturally responsive instructional supervision is as much an effort to change hearts as it is to change minds. Principals and teacher leaders must first focus on what efforts are necessary to influence the individual—which is at the core of any school improvement effort. In reviewing figure 4.2, the individual must change before more widespread improvement efforts can take place at the group level.

That being said, individuals can only grow so much on their own. Higher-order thinking, learning, and *changes in behavior* are most likely to occur when people share thoughts with one another and serve as co-learners to their cognitive development.[1] This can be seen when teachers support each other as critical colleagues—pairs or small groups of people who *chose their learning partners and trust each other enough to be vulnerable with their learning*. Over time, learning and growth can exponentially occur, at the individual level, within small groups, and eventually throughout the building across all faculty.

To learn in small groups, however, requires structure and trust to help teachers reflect on instruction and to deepen their own understanding of historical factors that influenced the development of US society and, as a result, the marginalization of groups that remain baked into the function of US society to this day. As such, critical colleagues should be people who help each other push their thinking about how instruction can lead to more equitable outcomes for all students. Through these groups, educators can challenge taken-for-granted assumptions about traditional approaches to education and learn how to implement culturally responsive instruction.

HOW CRITICAL COLLEAGUES HELP TO BETTER
UNDERSTAND THE SELF AND OTHERS

Becoming a CCRI involves instructional leadership creating critical col-league groups that offer teachers opportunities to learn and collaborate within small, intimate groups in real time. These groups can be formed within or across departments and school buildings, and instructional leadership plays a crucial role in their formation and support. There are several assumptions that adult learning groups should consider,[2] including

1. Members should be allowed to choose their groups and not be forced to take part in a group because of being assigned to a grade-level team or in a content-specific department. This will allow for learning to occur at more individualized rates.
2. Groups (suggested size is two to five people) can be modified and updated over time as determined by the group itself if it will help others learn and apply culturally responsive instructional practices. The repre-sentative supervision team can request teams fold in new members if it will help with growth, but it is ultimately the group's decision who is part of the group.
3. Group norms must be established prior to any learning. A good resource is to examine Johnson and Johnson[3] as a reference point to examining how high functioning groups address their work, conflict, and ulti-mately support each other to result in the outcome of learning together and supporting each other's growth. Good groups listen to each other, adapt norms over time, and use them as structures to promote learning.
4. The group determines and identifies personalized growth goals around culturally responsive instructional practices and asks for detailed sup-port and feedback about their efforts to implement culturally proficient practices.
5. The group supports an ongoing mindset about learning and supports each other in developing a critical consciousness about the ways in which teachers reflect upon their thinking about culturally responsive instruction and how it can be used in a liberatory manner to address marginalized experiences in the US school system.

By permitting teachers to form their own critical colleague groups, it is more likely that, over time, the process will be seen as authentic and that educators will be more willing to question notions of whether it is possible for education to be apolitical or ahistorical. Through ongoing discussions about culturally responsive instruction, critical colleagues can develop reflective stances about what inclusive instruction looks like and how it leads to a greater sense of belonging among all children, particularly those from minoritized, marginalized, and otherized groups.

Figure 3.2 helps reflect on what leads to changes in the subconscious and conscious regarding instructional practices. The culturally responsive instructional supervision self-study cycle takes time—and many discussions and interrogations of data from classroom observations—to change the teaching that occurs in a building. What results, eventually, is the application of more humanizing instruction.

Through the development of critical colleague groups, teachers support each other in ongoing formative feedback that helps them to continually center the voices and the experiences of the marginalized in US society. In this process, it is critical for these small groups of teachers to self-reflect on their own privileged identities but also help their colleagues reflect on their privileged identities as well. Through this process, educators can begin to realize how school systems marginalize and oppress students in a multitude of ways.[4] After this realization, educators can begin focusing on asset- and strength-based pedagogical approaches that acknowledge infinite ways to educate children.

TOPICS OF DISCUSSION FOR CRITICAL COLLEAGUE GROUPS

Through acts of love and support, teachers, teacher leaders, and principals can help create CCRIs that ensure all students are represented in the curriculum and through instruction enacted from one classroom to another. Engaging in critical colleague groups requires educators to critically analyze the curriculum and ensure representation across various sociocultural identities. This effort involves reimagining the historically reinforced curriculum in the US PK–12 public school system, which has centered White, Eurocentric, male perspectives.[5] Deconstructing these biases is a long-term process, as it requires changing (sub)conscious thoughts about what is taught.

Critical colleague groups will also need to engage in deep (and sometimes emotional) conversations about what is assessed and how grades are earned by students. All too often students are assessed in a summative manner, but the data is not used in a formative manner to drive learning for each student. Any time a grade is collected it should be tied to an objective, and that is then used as feedback for the student receiving the grade about what they know and what they still need to learn. Ultimately, it is the responsibility of a teacher engaging in culturally responsive instruction to use assessments in a way that is meaningful, authentic, and reasonable.

Learning in small groups is also crucial for peers to support each other about the grading process used across departments and teams. Critical colleagues can help each other create grading systems that are clear, supported by rubrics, and allow for creative application of knowledge to show understanding of learning objectives. If effort is something that needs to be communicated or expressed, that should be done separately and clearly noted as an "effort" grade that is different from a grade that reflects understanding. There are plenty of students that perform well on tests that lack effort—and critical colleagues can discuss how to keep these measurements separate.

How education systems create meaningful engagement with parents is another important topic for critical colleagues to engage in and discuss. This is particularly important for parents who come from historically marginalized groups that lacked culturally responsive experiences in school and/or parents who work hours outside the traditional school schedule. Teachers might work together to discuss how to coordinate parent activities with community-based groups and to collect feedback directly from parents about how they would like to be welcomed into the school as a way to discuss these efforts in order to improve parental engagement within critical colleague groups.

Central to any work that is labeled as culturally responsive is focusing on how to deepen engagement based on students' identities and lived experiences.[6] This includes reflecting on the number of children who have access to advanced coursework who identify as a marginalized group, providing instructional opportunities that address socioemotional well-being, and ensuring students of any background or economic means have the opportunity to be engaged in extracurricular activities. This requires deconstructing policies and practices that prevent the creation of equitable representation, as well as removing barriers to access participation (fees, transportation, necessary equipment).

While there are other topics to discuss, it is crucial that the group establish their own norms for how they will work together, as this will determine the success of each critical colleague group. A key component of this work is purposefully identifying individualized growth goals around culturally responsive instructional practices and the type of feedback that is requested *and* that is developmentally appropriate to facilitate learning. It is through supportive but difficult growth that a critical consciousness can be developed for culturally responsive teaching practices.

BEING PURPOSEFUL WITH DISCUSSIONS
TO DRIVE DIFFICULT GROWTH EDGES

First and foremost, feedback doesn't have to be difficult. In fact, if said from a place of love, as suggested that all culturally responsive instructional supervision is intended to be, the feedback can be seen as a way to support each other through what would be difficult growth if done individually and in isolation. When critical colleagues give feedback to one another, it should be done in a way that is seen as being given with love and received in a way that is seen as loving to help push thinking to promote more culturally responsive instructional practices.

It is also important to clarify that when a person shares an opinion about a belief or an instructional practice that is not culturally responsive, it doesn't have to signal that someone is "getting in trouble." Instead, these are the very moments of learning that are so often mislabeled as failures when they are the very work schools need to focus on to help produce culturally responsive practices. By having these discussions and engaging with critical colleagues, teachers can help close sociocultural gaps in a formative and constructive manner that is focused, supportive, and developmentally appropriate.

Ultimately, the goal of the work is to empower teachers to support each other to become guardians of culturally responsive teaching in a manner that is naturally inquisitive, nonoffensive, and signals a collective and ongoing improvement process. In doing so, teaching becomes deprivatized and celebrated. It should be a process that empowers teachers to engage in the liberation of the industrialized education system and to reconstruct education in a way that values constructive and supportive feedback about instruction.

Culturally responsive instructional supervision, particularly through critical colleagues, helps improve practices by not pointing out mistakes but rather developing collaboratively to develop more inclusive instruction. When the instructional supervision process flattens the hierarchy of feedback, an organic feedback system is created that increases the likelihood that culturally responsive practices are enacted. In other words, classroom teachers who receive formative feedback about their instruction should also be able to give feedback to other teachers about what they learn from the development of their reflective stances.

This is why it is so important for critical colleague groups to form on their own, as they will naturally assist in developing CCRIs and breaking down the siloed approach of traditional PLCs. In many ways, critical colleague groups are acts of resistance to the reinforcement of oppressive practices within the education system. These groups should meet because they have a natural interest in learning together—not because a system gave them a set task to accomplish.

For schools to put equity and inclusion at the center of instructional decisions requires deep, and sometimes difficult, conversations about how the accountability movement has largely failed communities and has done little to close the sociocultural gap in the United States.[7] Together, critical colleague groups can support each other, with empathy and love, to ensure public schools create learning opportunities for all students, not just those who are privileged. In doing so, educators can create structures that not only identify inequities but address them structurally.

USING EVERY GROUP CONVERSATION AS AN OPPORTUNITY TO DISCUSS EQUITY

This chapter provides a framework to improve upon the formative feedback loop that historically has plagued education systems—and thus practices— in US schools. Critical thinking about how and in what ways teachers can increase sense of belonging and inclusion through instructional practices can occur when new, more organic systems are in place to help instructors question assumptions about learning outcomes that are deficit oriented. By working with critical colleague groups, teachers retain their autonomy to develop more culturally responsive instruction as well as further develop a CCRI to address inequities that occur throughout the schoolhouse.

To help the formation of critical colleagues, the following are questions that groups should engage in and address to ensure formative feedback about the development of culturally responsive instructional practices occurs in a manner that is systematic and in a way that is intentional:

- Using resources to develop group norms (again, Johnson & Johnson[8] as an example is strongly suggested), what are the ground rules critical colleagues can come back to repeatedly to create groups that are organic, supportive, and focus on formative feedback that drives individual growth?
- How can critical colleague groups support the development of critical and sociocultural consciousness within teachers to create learning opportunities for students to address sociopolitical inequities that are rampant throughout US society?
- What can be learned from the team of intentionally representative instructional supervisors, and how might the formative feedback they provide about observed instructional practices be discussed and digested in smaller critical colleague groups?

- How might critical colleague groups be a safe place to discuss the data collected by the team of representative instructional supervisors, and what insights does the collected data have for how teachers reflect (and improve upon) their own instructional practices?
- How might smaller groups of critical colleagues provide safe places to unpack, discuss, and address how privileged identities can become decentered through daily instruction in a school?
- What are other methods of data collection that can be developed in small critical colleague groups that can be used to examine instructional inequities and how might these evolve in a democratic fashion to become used across groups and eventually across a school building?
- What does "good instruction" look like in a classroom that values culturally responsive instruction? How does this vary by developmental needs across grade levels in a way that challenges assumptions about deficit-oriented approaches to learning?[9]
- How might critical colleagues continually (re)position themselves to ensure the feedback provided among small groups is seen as loving and a tool for growth rather than a weapon to instill fear when an observed teaching practice or belief appears to lack cultural responsiveness?

The next chapter provides a framework for the final implementation of culturally responsive instructional supervision, where learning evolves from the individual level (i.e., self), beyond the small critical colleague group level and eventually spreads throughout an entire school building. Although the work is never truly "done," in this last stage teachers begin to apply what they have learned across departments, teams, and other school-based structures to apply skills and knowledge through peer-led classroom observations. The goal, ultimately, is to promote equitable instructional outcomes through peer feedback to inform ongoing cycles of inquiry.

NOTES

1. Stoll, L., Bolam, R., McMahon, A., Wallace, M., & Thomas, S. (2006). Professional learning communities: A review of the literature. *Journal of Educational Change, 7*, 221–258.

2. Merriam, S. B, & Bierema, L. L. (2014). *Adult learning: Linking theory and practice*. Jossey-Bass.

3. Johnson, D., & Johnson, F. (2016). *Joining together: Group theory and group skills* (12th ed.). Pearson.

4. Çevik, S., Yıldırım, S., & Zepeda, S. J. (2020). Leadership for socially-just supervision in K–12 schools in the context of the United States. *Multicultural Education Review, 12*(4), 306–322.

5. Carter Andrews, D. J., He, Y., Marciano, J. E., Richmond, G., & Salazar, M. (2021). Decentering whiteness in teacher education: Addressing the questions of who, with whom, and how. *Journal of Teacher Education, 72*(2), 134–137.

6. Khalifa, M. (2020). *Culturally responsive school leadership* (4th ed.). Harvard Education Press.

7. Radd, S. I., Generett, G. G., Gooden, M. A., & Theoharis, G. (2021). *Five practices for equity-focused school leadership*. ASCD.

8. Johnson, D., & Johnson, F. (2016). *Joining together: Group theory and group skills* (12th ed.). Pearson.

9. Bertrand, M., & Marsh, J. (2021). How data-driven reform can drive deficit thinking. *Phi Delta Kappan, 102*(8), 35–39.

Chapter 10

Using Peer-Led Classroom Observations to Drive Equitable Outcomes

Feedback from peer-led observations can be an incredibly powerful tool. It is a foundational reason why this framework uses a team of representative instructional supervisors constructed from teacher leaders throughout a group of faculty members. When feedback is provided from peers, professionals are more likely to see the feedback as valid and are far more likely to resist feedback if it comes from an administrator who either doesn't have content expertise or who is seen as disconnected from the realities of the everyday classroom.[1] And it is for this reason that peer-led observations can be powerful tools to drive instructional improvement.

While they can be incredibly important ways to help implement culturally responsive practices, there is certainly an art and a science to consider prior to engaging in peer-led observations. The main difference between the feedback offered in critical colleague groups and the feedback provided in peer-led observations is that peer-led observations are intended (a) to be content/grade level specific (organized by teams or departments), (b) to be mandatory (not chosen by individuals), and (c) to replicate the observation process that generates data similar to what is provided in tables 6.1, 6.2, and 6.3. In many ways, it is a train-the-trainer model.

While teams and departments will choose different rates and times when to engage in the peer-led observation process, it is critical that they embark in the work in a manner that continues to value trust and vulnerability and, above all, is conducted with love and support. Peers will not be open to feedback if the observations are seen as intrusive or a vehicle to register what might feel like unfair critique of teaching practices. Moreover, teams and departments will need to establish ground rules about how and when observations should occur and empower the teacher being observed to establish background about personal goals they have set to help improve their instruction.[2]

First, teams or departments should begin by establishing ground rules or team norms to the peer-led observation process. These should be specific to the needs of the group of educators in each individual team or department and as such will vary across a school building. Prior to each scheduled observation, teams should review these rules to ensure both the observer and the observed understand the agreed-upon process and objectives, as noted by other systems that establish parameters for collecting data across a building.[3] Doing so prevents any misunderstandings, which is critical in creating a CCRI that is based on trust, vulnerability, and the belief that through formative feedback instructional practices can improve.

Second, team-based or department-based observations should be scheduled in a way that allows those conducting the observation to leverage their content expertise as a central aspect of the feedback. This should be done to help the person being observed see the feedback as valid based on the knowledge and training of the observer. Scheduling observations in this way also values pedagogical practices that are developmentally appropriate and developmental-centric.

Third, each team or department should create a form, approved by all members, that can easily be completed and presented to the observed teacher before the end of the day of the observation. This can be a paper or electronic form, but it should be aligned with school goals to increase culturally responsive instruction and any individual goals set by the teacher being observed. Again, educators should refer to tables 6.1, 6.2, and 6.3 to inform the observation process by the team of intentionally representative instructional supervisors that generates similar data. An example of what a peer-led observation form might entail is provided in figure 10.1.

Fourth, teams or departments should use the peer-led observation process to engage in discussions with one another about what was observed and how the observation helped reflect on instructional practices.[4] These discussions can occur in informal spaces—such as in the hallway, in the teacher's lounge, or in the parking lot—or they can occur in formal spaces such as team or department meetings where part of the agenda is dedicated to these reflections. Whatever the group decides is most valuable and helps drive improvement for culturally responsive instructional practices is what should happen.

Ultimately, the goal of the peer-led observation process is for educators to *apply their learning about how they are becoming more culturally responsive in a structured way* that helps them see the bigger organizational picture about how inequities are addressed in their school building. From these observations, teachers will have deeper reflections on what they are learning, as well as how they are being encouraged to grow—and how they can better

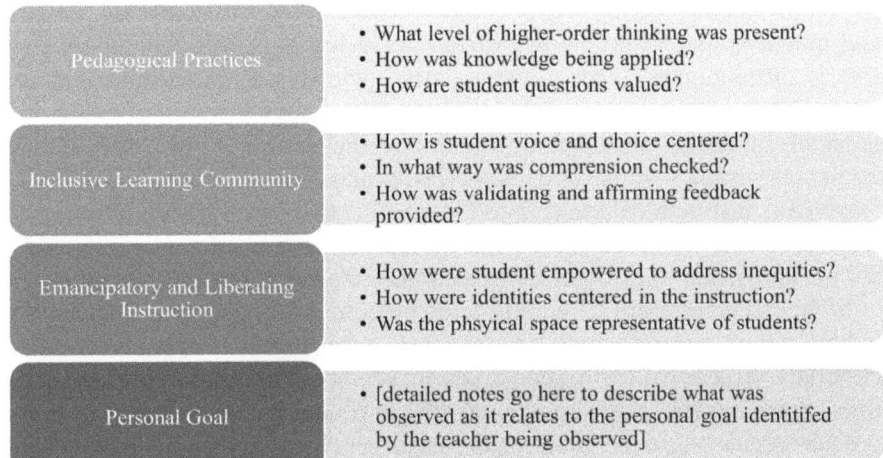

Pedagogical Practices	• What level of higher-order thinking was present? • How was knowledge being applied? • How are student questions valued?
Inclusive Learning Community	• How is student voice and choice centered? • In what way was comprension checked? • How was validating and affirming feedback provided?
Emancipatory and Liberating Instruction	• How were student empowered to address inequities? • How were identities centered in the instruction? • Was the phsyical space representative of students?
Personal Goal	• [detailed notes go here to describe what was observed as it relates to the personal goal identitifed by the teacher being observed]

Figure 10.1.   Example of Peer-Led Observation Form

encourage others—in their critical colleague group. Below we detail how reflections can connect across an entire school.

HOW PEER WALKTHROUGHS CAN HELP CALIBRATE BUILDING-WIDE EXPECTATIONS

From the data that is collected and the conversations about what is observed across teams and departments, teachers can have conversations about setting team-based or department-based goals. These goals should focus on improving one aspect of culturally responsive instruction at a time, and they are likely best suited to be established goals that can be measured and reflected upon one quarter or trimester at a time. As the needs of the department evolve, so will the goals, which might focus on increasing student voice one quarter/trimester and change to focus on ensuring the physical space is representative of students the next quarter/trimester.

In addition to setting team- or department-level goals, peed-led observations can be used to help consider setting schoolwide goals that can be used to drive improvement efforts for inclusion.[5] During faculty-wide meetings, teachers can share out observations and reflections based on collected observational data and engage in conversations about what they believe the school should focus on to improve implementation of culturally responsive instructional strategies. This can be a useful strategy in helping calibrate building-wide expectations about the use of formative data as it relates to supervision cycles.

Part of establishing these expectations is solidifying and codifying policies and practices that value the use of formative feedback through supervision that is differentiated from the summative practices of evaluation that are related to human resource decisions.[6] As stated earlier, teacher evaluation is legally required and plays an important role in determining who should be in classrooms with children and who should not be. However, culturally responsive instructional supervision is practice that can and should occur on an almost daily basis about how factors such as race, gender, ethnicity, SES, ability, and spatiality influence instruction in the US education system.

What can come from a building-wide process where people are constantly talking about, and reflecting on, feedback regarding the implementation of culturally responsive instructional practices is a culture that values the continual measurement of the implementation of pedagogy. Individually, in small critical colleague groups, in teams or departments, and across an entire school building, teachers should always have on the tip of their tongue and at the front of their brain thoughts about how to make instruction more equitable and inclusive.[7] It is from this process that the culture of a building can be changed and improved over time.

USING PEER FEEDBACK TO INFORM INQUIRY CYCLES

The hope of the culturally responsive instructional supervision framework is to develop a system that, over time, creates teams and departments that can independently collect data about, and reflect upon, instructional practices without needing the representative instructional supervision team. As an example, teams or departments could focus on collecting data about validating and affirming feedback (see figure 6.2 as an example) and begin to ask themselves the following questions:

- How might we connect students to a deeper understanding of the learning objective?
- What are the broad cultural connections that will help students be more interested in applying knowledge to the learning objective?
- How can we differentiate learning to reflect the sociocultural identities of our students?

As with any school improvement effort, there will always be resistance to change. However, by leveraging expertise of teacher leaders and forming a representative instructional supervision team, valuing autonomy to grow at the individual level, supporting critical colleague groups that learn together and at their own pace, and distributing accountability across teams and departments to provide feedback based on peer-led observations, schools can lead themselves in the process of developing into more equitable education systems. Working in this way allows individuals *and* the structures they inherit to push past resistance to drive equitable improvement.

What this framework also attempts to do is strike a balance between inquiry cycles that center the individual and place value in determining group decisions. The reality is that both are important and necessary if the US education system is to enact change regarding the function of society and the outcomes of social systems within US society. Schools need more structures and support systems that help teachers understand the lived experiences of marginalized students but also to rethink and reimagine more broadly education systems that discriminate in a variety of ways against students due to a plethora of deficit-based approaches to instruction.

To become an asset-based education system will require unabashed dismantling of what we have come to accept from the US PK–12 education system and require acts of resistance from educators who know there is something better than what is currently offered. If schools can make this shift by showing they are accountable to the students and parents they serve, they should have enough support to construct a system that is loving, caring, and accepting of individuals from all backgrounds and identities. The work starts with principals and teacher leaders—but it requires leadership at the classroom level as well—to engage in changed instructional practices.[8]

TRANSFORMING FEEDBACK ACROSS A SCHOOL TO DECONSTRUCT SYSTEMS OF INEQUITY

Once a culture of feedback is accepted and imbedded in practices across a school building, faculty members can work across teams and departments to not only enact change, but also to systematically address inequities through culturally responsive instructional practices. At every level, educators can work on improving themselves and the system—within the self, within small groups, and within the schoolhouse more broadly. Over time, discussing and addressing inequities becomes just another example of "how we do things around here," where educators actively engage in acts of resistance to combat practices and policies that marginalize students and parents.

Referring back to figure 8.1, there is a continual process to eliminating instructional inequities that can occur across a school. Through this work, educators across a building continually engage in the process of identifying what outcomes create disparities among groups of students that are inequitable. These can be addressed through large sets of observational data collected by the intentionally representative instructional supervision team that represent what is occurring across a building, or in smaller data sets that examine how instruction varies across teams or departments.

Once inequitable outcomes have been identified, educators can work collaboratively to develop a plan for how to address the disparities and remediate them. These inequities may include pedagogical practices that are predominantly lower-order thinking, lack student voice and input into the learning process, or reinforce deficit-oriented practices that fail to center identities and lived experiences. In developing these plans, educators should discuss how others might provide higher-order thinking investigations, center student voice into how the learning is applied, or make a shift toward asset-based learning.

After a plan is made, either as a team or department, or even across an entire school building, educators need to implement the actions needed to address and eliminate the instructional inequities. Accountability structures can be created, including self-assessments that help individual teachers reflect on the instructional improvement plan or receiving feedback from critical colleague groups with pinpointed feedback about targeted areas of improvement. Over the course of several weeks, the instructional supervision team can collect several hundred data points that determine if progress has been made.

Perhaps most important, teachers, instructional supervisors, and principals will need to work together to assess if the effort worked, if they need more time to determine if it worked, or if a different approach needs to occur to make sure improvements are made. The continuous improvement cycle then repeats itself, likely resulting in setting new goals. Over time, these instructional goals are measured and reflected upon, and then a determination is made as to whether further intervention is needed or if new goals can be set. The process then continues indefinitely.

ALLOWING INSTRUCTIONAL IMPROVEMENT EFFORTS TO EVOLVE OVER TIME FOR MORE EQUITABLE OUTCOMES

Discussing schoolwide efforts to increase inclusive instruction is not as straightforward as some educators might hope. It requires intense planning and ongoing review of structures that even the best leaders will struggle to implement because it is such a sharp departure from what has been measured and deemed important since the inception of NCLB. It also means that principals will need to empower teacher leaders to engage in this work in a way that has not been traditionally valued and will require a "power with" approach rather than a "power over" approach.

Due to these factors, the implementation of a culturally responsive instructional supervision system across an entire school building requires resources. Teachers will need time, support, and encouragement to unlearn how schools operate as systems of oppression for students who are marginalized, minoritized, and otherized. Developing teacher leaders who can implement the supervision team process and collect data consistently and accurately will need time as well. The process and progress are more likely to be measured in years than in months.

Along the way, principals will need to rethink how common meeting time is used, both in faculty meetings and in team or department meetings, to engage in this work in a deep and thoughtful manner. How information is shared will need to change, meaning that announcements that can be shared through written form can be sent through emails and that faculty should be prepared to adjust for this change.

In doing so, large chunks of time can be opened up to support the learning of teams and departments, as well as across the entire school building, to reflect, discuss, disagree, become frustrated, have "ah-ha" moments, and evolve into a supportive CCRI that creates more equitable instructional outcomes for all students. Due to the individualized and organic nature of the culturally responsive instructional supervision framework, some critical colleague groups and teams/departments will learn much faster than others.

Without question this will create tension within teacher ranks and will require instructional leaders who can facilitate the development of equity-minded teachers who can become aware of, and then address, the inequities that occur within a school building.[9] In many ways, the different rates of growth and development of implementing culturally responsive instructional practices will help teachers see why it is so important for them to use asset-based approaches in their own classrooms.

Perhaps most important, educational leaders will need to remember that this is a formative learning process and that over time the goal is to transform belief systems of individuals who can then transform the system. This framework is not something that should be used for summative teacher evaluation purposes as the ability to grow into a culturally responsive instructor is built on the notion of trust and vulnerability. Teachers will make mistakes in becoming culturally responsive—and sometimes they will be big mistakes—but without struggle there can be no gain, and children in the United States desperately need educators to engage in this work.

NOTES

1. Fusarelli, L. D., & Fusarelli, B. C. (2019). Instructional supervision in an era of high-stakes accountability (pp. 131–158). In S. J. Zepeda & J. A. Ponticell (Eds.), *The Wiley Handbook of educational supervision*. John Wiley & Sons, Inc.

2. Johnson, D., & Johnson, F. (2016). *Joining together: Group theory and group skills* (12th ed.). Pearson.

3. Valentine, J. (2009). *The instructional practices inventory: Using a student learning assessment to foster organizational learning*. National Staff Development Council, Annual Convention, St. Louis, MO.

4. Kachur, D. S., Stout, J. A., & Edwards, C. L. (2013). *Classroom walkthroughs to improve teaching and learning* (2nd ed.). Routledge.

5. Ezzani, M. D. (2019). Principal and teacher instructional leadership: A cultural shift. *International Journal of Educational Management, 34*(3), 576–585.

6. Glickman, C. D., Gordon, S. P., & Ross-Gordon, J. M. (2018). *Supervision and instructional leadership: A developmental approach* (10th ed.). Pearson.

7. Radd, S. I., Generett, G. G., Gooden, M. A., & Theoharis, G. (2021). *Five practices for equity-focused school leadership*. ASCD.

8. Khalifa, M. (2020). *Culturally responsive school leadership* (4th ed.). Harvard Education Press.

9. Cooper, K. S., Stanulis, R. N., Brondyk, S. K., Hamilton, E. R., Mascaluso, M., & Meier, J. A. (2018). The teacher leadership process: Attempting change within embedded systems. *Journal of Educational Change, 17*, 85–113.

Chapter 11

Conclusion

Signaling a Shift in Where We Must Go

Instructional leaders, principals, and teacher leaders alike need to be prepared to help educators adapt to the needs of historically marginalized students in the twenty-first century and be prepared to address ongoing inequities that have been perpetuated through the evolution of US society. Waiting for state or federal governments to make decisions on behalf of the oppressed is not a valid solution—and in fact, school leaders must be willing to actively resist oppressive state-level policies that prevent addressing inequities. It is in this spirit—for the betterment of *all people* in US society—that we provide this framework.

To enact culturally responsive instructional supervision requires leaders to engage in the process of "a radical moral imagination"[1] (p. 238) to acknowledge and address the ills of White supremacy, anti-Blackness, xenophobia, homophobia, transphobia, elitism, and ableism, among others, in a head-on and direct manner. The US education system has never been apolitical or ahistorical, and children in the United States deserve to see education as a pathway to address the immoral beliefs and actions of social systems in their country. This requires that all educators develop commitment to instruction that demands equality, inclusion, and belonging.

Feedback about instruction, although often ignored by modern school improvement efforts, is the most direct way to improve outcomes for children. When teachers use approaches that value the sociocultural identities of students, as well as their lived experiences, it allows them to see themselves in the classroom but also make connections between each other and how they might work to support each other in an egalitarian society. All of this can occur, but it must be through concrete data collected about instruction, as well as through feedback cycles that value the development of reflective stances that focuses on equitable outcomes for all students.

RESISTING TECHNORATIONAL APPROACHES
TO IMPROVING INSTRUCTION

Part of what must occur is that principals—educators who are supposed to be the instructional leaders of the building—need to signal a shift away from hardcore teacher evaluation practices that have reinforced the idea that there is one right way to teach children. These approaches, often reinforced by systems like Marzano and Danielson, reinforce deficit-minded approaches to teaching that center the voice of the privileged, fail to question the sociocultural identities of teachers and how that influences their approaches to teaching, and seek to affirm hierarchical power of school systems. In short, they see teachers and students as people to be controlled.

The current high-stakes teacher evaluation policy in the United States creates a management system that empowers the principal as overseer and enforcer of these deficit-minded instructional strategies. It provides an opportunity for a person of power to assert control over what is taught, how it is taught, and who it is taught for. When local or state education systems use policy to prevent or deny social power or privilege, there is a continuation of the sociocultural gap. When this happens, inequities remain unaddressed, accepted, and seen as the accepted norm by educators, often biased toward privileged racial, class, and gender identities.

Instead, instructional leaders, who include teacher leaders with content expertise, need to help signal a shift toward feedback about instruction that values sociocultural identities. This feedback should center the voices and experiences of the marginalized, minoritized, and otherized. It should also help educators reflect on their own privileges—as well as any marginalized experiences they may have had in school or society more broadly—in a way that helps reimagine what school can be. At the heart of this work is making a pivot toward asset-based pedagogies that see identities as a strength and acknowledges there are infinite ways to educate children.

Additionally, principals and teacher leaders need to help building cultures move beyond the infatuation with technocratic measurement of teacher effectives that is highly aligned with producing results on standardized tests.[2] While standardized tests are one way to measure intelligence, they are also highly flawed with the belief that achievement should be distributed on a bell curve, and they also are shown to be discriminatory toward students of color. As such, instructional supervisors need to honor the expertise of culturally responsive teachers and help develop alternative measures to determine teacher effectiveness.

To break free of controlling teacher evaluation systems that are a form of workplace behaviorism,[3] instructional supervisors need to point toward measurements of teacher evaluation that can include student portfolios, apply student projects to social outcomes in their community, use student and parent surveys, and develop other metrics that can improve how teachers reflect on the instruction they provide *in the name of producing equity-based learning opportunities*. Moving past plantation practices that attempt to control the minds of teachers and students is critical if the US education system is to help our society move beyond its violent past.

USING SUPERVISION TO SUPPORT
A SYSTEM OF OPPORTUNITY

To move beyond technorational approaches to instructional supervision, principals need to use the distributive leadership approach of creating an intentionally representative supervision team that leverages the instructional expertise of teacher leaders throughout the building. Creating a team like this helps ensure feedback from a variety of people with various perspectives about culturally responsive practices. The hope, over time, is that teachers can reflect on observational data and have peer-to-peer conversations about how they can ensure students see themselves through inclusive instructional practices.

Through a variety of structures that can be relatively easy and inexpensive to implement, instructional supervisors can provide opportunities to reflect on their (sub)conscious beliefs that impede the development of cultural competence. These structures include collecting hundreds of observational data points and empowering teachers to unpack what the data means and to target opportunities for improvement. It also means developing a plan of action when instruction is not culturally responsive and providing developmentally appropriate feedback for further reflection. From these structures, teachers can participate in how to implement school improvement.

At its core, culturally responsive instructional supervision is a developmental approach that values (1) self-reflection and (2) growth with critical colleagues. Both of these support teachers engaging in formative feedback structures that involve critical self-reflection and how education systems perpetuate inequities and privileges if not directly acknowledged and addressed. It is through critical self-reflection that adults are able to engage in transformational learning that influences beliefs and practices,[4] something that instructional supervisors must reinforce with teachers to help increase dialogue about culturally responsive instructional practices.

HONORING "GETTING INTO GOOD TROUBLE"

As schools engage in the work of bridging the gap between culturally respon-sive teaching[5] and culturally responsive school leadership,[6] culturally respon-sive instructional supervision should focus on the autonomy of teachers to develop at their own pace *as well as* removing the fear that trying something that addresses equity will result in "getting in trouble." Instead, educational leaders need to support the idea of getting into good trouble—particularly as educators break free from the failed accountability experiment that started with NCLB. This requires acts of resistance to practices that are oppressive and exclusionary.

To engage in this type of learning means that instructional supervisors need to honor the importance of teachers reflecting in their own self-collected data, feedback received from peers, and eventually feedback from peer-led obser-vations. From this type of reflection, teachers can consider action research projects about instructional practices that address the needs of the community they serve. As long as a teacher engages in meeting the needs of a commu-nity and is being inclusive of the sociocultural identities of their students, there should be nothing controversial about efforts to improve instructional practices.

As such, one of the main jobs of a culturally responsive instructional super-visor is to celebrate and support the autonomy of teachers. There is nothing more important than protecting the instructional practices of teachers to become more self-critical and reflect on how more equitable outcomes might occur through classroom instruction. Once teachers start working on growing as an individual, they can branch out and learn in small groups, which should result in a whole other level of learning where educators learn to question, together, inequities that occur within their school system.

At its most basic form, educators should never be afraid to address dis-parities in instruction, especially those that are supported by data. Over time, instructional supervisors should be able to empower teachers to resist the tra-ditions of oppressive education systems and focus on developing asset-based teaching practices that help make instruction more inclusive and meaningful. Reimagining a Eurocentric curriculum, ensuring marginalized students have access to advanced coursework, and welcoming the voices of marginalized students and parents as pieces of feedback are all examples of reflective activities that must be protected by instructional leaders.

A CLOSING NOTE TO PRACTITIONERS

This book is meant to serve as a handbook—a roadmap of sorts—to help principals and teacher leaders develop culturally responsive instructional supervision strategies and practices in their schools and districts. We can no longer afford to think about instructional feedback coming from just the principal or just a reading or math coach, but rather we must think systemically about how we *all* reflect on instructional practices. Worse yet, we can no longer allow "feedback" to be dominated by summative teacher evaluation that does not lead to more inclusive instruction.

Prior to implementing the suggested strategies, however, we recommend reading this book several times before implementing any of the proposed framework. School leaders need to think deeply about their commitment to reflecting on instructional strategies, and it will take time and planning to successfully launch a new paradigm around formative feedback about developing culturally responsive instruction. We want to reiterate that rethinking and reimagining supervisory feedback to produce more equitable outcomes for all students will take time and will not be a quick fix—to address systemic issues that we see about instruction in the United States will take years.

This book provides a framework for thinking about culturally responsive instructional supervision and is not a prescribed method. It is of the utmost importance that all schools, collaboratively, develop their own ways of providing feedback about instructional practices so that culturally responsive instruction can flourish at the individual and building level. While we hope to develop a system in the future that can help deliver on the promise of a formalized culturally responsive instructional supervision system, right now it simply does not exist. As such, practitioners and researchers will need to work together to create these in the years to come.

It is also important for people to remember that data is a tool for improvement. It is a way to share feedback about instruction that provides support and love for both teachers and the students they teach. Contrary to the way most teacher evaluation systems use it, data is not a tool to promote fear and is not a weapon to drive change. Data about observed instructional practices is intended to help teachers reflect, set improvement goals, grow as more culturally responsive instructors, and create an education system that focuses on asset-based pedagogies as well as honors and values the identities students bring to the classroom each and every day.

As part of the ongoing development of culturally responsive instructional supervision, we strongly encourage practitioners to crowdsource ideas, practices, and development of groups to help others grow as educators, implement school improvement efforts, and change in terms of more equitable outcomes for all students. Please share templates and observation tools with others and do so in a way that celebrates reflective practices about inclusive instruction. The education system will not change if we operate in isolation and if we perpetuate the siloed approaches we have failed to reconceptualize from previous school improvement efforts.

It is important to form your coalitions. Bring together people from a wide variety of sociocultural identities. Even those with multiple privileged identities have been marginalized by the education system at some point in their lives. Use those experiences to develop empathy for the students and parents your school system is intended to serve. And then act on the empathy. Realize you can change the experiences students have in your community. But perhaps most important, approach the work with love for children. US society cannot move forward and be equitable until the schoolhouse is a safe, inclusive, and equitable place for all of us.

NOTES

1. Laymon, K. (2018). *Heavy: An American memoir*. Scribner.

2. Mette, I. M., Aguilar, I., & Wieczorek, D. (2020). A thirty state analysis of teacher supervision and evaluation systems in the ESSA era. *Journal of Educational Supervision, 3*(2), 105–135.

3. Hazi, H. M. (2019). Coming to understand the wicked problem of teacher evaluation. In S. J. Zepeda & J. A. Ponticell (Eds.), *The Wiley handbook of educational supervision* (pp. 183–208). Wiley Blackwell.

4. Mezirow, J. (2009). Transformative learning theory. In J. Mezirow & E. W. Taylor (Eds.), *Transformative learning in practice: Insights from community, workplace, and higher education* (pp. 18–32). Jossey-Bass.

5. Gay, G. (2018). *Culturally responsive teaching: Theory, research, and practice* (2nd ed.). Teachers College Press.

6. Khalifa, M. (2020). *Culturally responsive school leadership* (4th ed.). Harvard Education Press.

Bibliography

Alim, H. S., & Paris, D. (2017). What is culturally sustaining pedagogy and why does it matter? In D. Paris & H. S. Alim (Eds.), *Teaching and learning for justice in a changing world* (pp. 1–24). Teachers College Press.

ASCD. (2019). Confronting the crisis of educational inequity. *Educational Leadership, 14*(23). https://www.ascd.org/el/articles/confronting-the-crisis-of-education-inequity

Bertrand, M., & Marsh, J. (2021). How data-driven reform can drive deficit thinking. *Phi Delta Kappan, 102*(8), 35–39.

Bustillo, X. (2022). Who and what is behind abortion ban trigger law bills? Two groups laid the groundwork. *National Public Radio.* https://www.npr.org/2022/07/08/1110299496/trigger-laws-13-states-two-groups-laid-groundwork

Carter Andrews, D. J., He, Y., Marciano, J. E., Richmond, G., & Salazar, M. (2021). Decentering whiteness in teacher education: Addressing the questions of who, with whom, and how. *Journal of Teacher Education, 72*(2), 134–137.

Çevik, S., Yıldırım, S., & Zepeda, S. J. (2020). Leadership for socially-just supervision in K–12 schools in the context of the United States. *Multicultural Education Review, 12*(4), 306–322.

Cooper, K. S., Stanulis, R. N., Brondyk, S. K., Hamilton, E. R., Mascaluso, M., & Meier, J. A. (2018). The teacher leadership process: Attempting change within embedded systems. *Journal of Educational Change, 17*, 85–113.

Cormier, D. R. (2021). Assessing preservice teachers' cultural competence with the cultural proficiency continuum q-sort. *Educational Researcher, 50*(1), 17–29.

Cormier, D. R. (2022). Prototyping the Cultural Proficiency Continuum Dialogic Protocol with professional development school teacher interns. *Urban Education.* https://doi.org/10.1177/00420859221140405

Cormier, D. R., & Pandey, T. (2021). Semiotic analysis of a foundational textbook used widely across educational supervision. *Journal of Educational Supervision, 4*(2), 101–132.

Dolan, T., Christens, B. D., & Lin, C. (2015). Combining youth organization and youth participatory action research to strengthen student voice in education reform. *Teachers College Record, 117*(13), 153–170.

Duarte, B. J. (2020). Forced back into the closet: A (queer) principal's attempt to maintain queer erasure. *Journal of Cases in Educational Leadership, 23*(4), 20–34.

Ezzani, M. D. (2019). Principal and teacher instructional leadership: A cultural shift. *International Journal of Educational Management, 34*(3), 576–585.

Fisher-Ari, T. R., Speights, R., Veazie, M., Haile, H., Tennies, E., & Ngo, H. (2020). Organizational cultural competence in PDS networks and teacher certification programs. In J. Ferrara, J. L. Nath, & R. S. Beebe, *Exploring cultural competence in professional development schools* (pp. 1–25). Information Age Publishing.

Freire, P. (1970). *Pedagogy of the oppressed.* Seabury Press.

Fusarelli, L. D., & Fusarelli, B. C. (2019). Instructional supervision in an era of high-stakes accountability (pp. 131–158). In S. J. Zepeda & J. A. Ponticell (Eds.), *The Wiley Handbook of educational supervision.* John Wiley & Sons, Inc.

Gay, G. (2018). *Culturally responsive teaching: Theory, research, and practice* (2nd ed.). Teachers College Press.

Givens, J. (2021). *Fugitive pedagogy: Carter G. Woodson and the art of Black teaching.* Harvard University Press.

Glickman, C. D., Gordon, S. P., & Ross-Gordon, J. M. (2018). *Supervision and instructional leadership: A developmental approach* (10th ed.). Pearson.

Glickman, C. D., & Mette, I. M. (2020). *The essential renewal of America's schools: A leadership guide for democratizing schools from the inside out.* Teachers College Press.

Gooden, M. A., & Dantley, M. (2012). Centering race in a framework for leadership preparation. *Journal of Research on Leadership Education, 7*(2), 237–253.

Grissom, J. A., & Bartanen, B. (2018). Strategic retention: Principal effectiveness and teacher turnover in multiple-measure teacher evaluation systems. *American Educational Research Journal*, 1–42. https://doi.org/10.3102/0002831218797931

Guerra, P. L., Baker, A. M., & Cotman, A. (2022). Instructional supervision: Is it culturally responsive? A textbook analysis. *Journal of Educational Supervision, 5*(1), 1–26. https://doi.org/10.31045/jes.5.1.1

Hazi, H. M. (2019). Coming to understand the wicked problem of teacher evaluation. In S. J. Zepeda & J. A. Ponticell (Eds.), *The Wiley handbook of educational supervision* (pp. 183–208). Wiley Blackwell.

Irby, D. J. (2021). *Stuck improving: Racial equity and school leadership.* Harvard Education Press.

Jay, M. (2003). Critical race theory, multicultural education, and the hidden curriculum of hegemony. *Multicultural Perspectives, 5*(4), 3–9.

Johnson, D., & Johnson, F. (2016). *Joining together: Group theory and group skills* (12th ed.). Pearson.

Kachur, D. S., Stout, J. A., & Edwards, C. L. (2013). *Classroom walkthroughs to improve teaching and learning* (2nd ed.). Routledge.

Kendi, I. X. (2021). Our new postracial myth. *The Atlantic.* https://www.theatlantic.com/ideas/archive/2021/06/our-new-postracial-myth/619261/

Khalifa, M. (2020). *Culturally responsive school leadership* (4th ed.). Harvard Education Press.

Krathwohl, D. R. (2002). A revision of Bloom's taxonomy: An overview. *Theory into Practice, 41*(4), 212–218.

Ladson-Billings, G. (1998). Just what is critical race theory and what's it doing in a nice field like education? *Qualitative Studies in Education, 11*(1), 7–24.

Ladson-Billings, G. (1999). Preparing teachers for diverse student populations: A critical race theory perspective. *Review of Research in Education, 24*, 211–247.

Ladson-Billings, G. (2017). The (r)evolution will not be standardized. In D. Paris & H. S. Alim (Eds.), *Culturally sustaining pedagogies: Teaching and learning for justice in a changing world* (pp. 141–156). Teachers College Press.

Lam, K. D. (2015). Teaching for liberation: Critical reflections in teacher education. *Multicultural Perspectives, 17*(3), 157–162.

Laymon, K. (2018). *Heavy: An American memoir*. Scribner.

Lindsey, R. B., Robins, K. N., & Terrell, R. D. (2009). *Cultural proficiency: A manual for school leaders.* Corwin.

López, F. A. (2017). Altering the trajectory of the self-fulfilling prophecy: Asset-based pedagogy and classroom dynamics. *Journal of Teacher Education, 68*(2), 193–212.

Love, B. L. (2019a). Dear White teachers: You can't love your Black students if you don't know them. *Education Week, 38*(26), 18.

Love, B. L. (2019b). *We want to do more than survive: Abolitionist teaching and the pursuit of educational reform*. Beacon Press.

Lutton, L. (2012). Japanese strategy for improving teachers is catching on in Chicago. *The Hechinger Report*. https://hechingerreport.org/japanese-strategy-for -improving-teachers-is-catching-on-in-chicago/

Merriam, S. B, & Bierema, L. L. (2014). *Adult learning: Linking theory and practice*. Jossey-Bass.

Mette, I. M., Aguilar, I., & Wieczorek, D. (2020). A thirty state analysis of teacher supervision and evaluation systems in the ESSA era. *Journal of Educational Supervision, 3*(2), 105–135.

Mette, I. M., Range, B. G., Anderson, J., Hvidston, D. J., Nieuwenhuizen, L, & Doty, J. (2017). The wicked problem of the intersection between supervision and evaluation. *International Electronic Journal of Elementary Education, 9*(3), 709–724.

Mezirow, J. (2009). Transformative learning theory. In J. Mezirow & E. W. Taylor (Eds.), *Transformative learning in practice: Insights from community, workplace, and higher education* (pp. 18–32). Jossey-Bass.

Mills, C. W. (1997). *The racial contract*. Cornell University Press.

Milner IV, H. R. (2007). Race, culture, and researcher positionality: Working through dangers seen, unseen, and unforeseen. *Educational Researcher, 36*(7), 388–400.

Milner IV, H. R. (2008). Critical race theory and interest convergence as analytic tools in teacher education policies and practices. *Journal of Teacher Education, 59*(4), 332–346.

Milner IV, H. R. (2017). Where's the race in culturally relevant pedagogy? *Teachers College Record, 119*, 1–32.

Milner IV, H. R. (2020). *Start where you are, but don't stay there: Understanding diversity, opportunity gaps, and teaching in today's classrooms* (2nd ed.). Harvard Education Press.

Moss, C. M., Brookhart, S. M., & Long, B. A. (2013). Administrators' roles in helping teachers use formative assessment information. *Applied Measurement in Education, 26*(3), 205–218.

Muhammad, G. (2020). *Cultivating genius: An equity framework for culturally and historically responsive literacy.* Scholastic.

Muhammad, G. (2022). On identity. *Voices From the Middle, 30*(1), 14–16.

National Center for Education Statistics (NCES). (2016). Characteristics of public school teachers. https://nces.ed.gov/programs/coe/indicator_clr.asp

National Center for Education Statistics (NCES). (2017). *2017 Digest of Education Statistics.* https://nces.ed.gov/programs/digest/d16/tables/dt16_236.10.asp?current =yes

Oliveira, S., Roberto, M. S., Veiga-Simão, A. M., & Marques-Pinto, A. (2021). A meta-analysis of the impact of social and emotional learning interventions on teachers' burnout symptoms. *Educational Psychology Review, 33*(4), 1779–1808.

Pateman, C. (1998). *The sexual contract.* Stanford University Press.

Radd, S. I., Generett, G. G., Gooden, M. A., & Theoharis, G. (2021). *Five practices for equity-focused school leadership.* ASCD.

Schwartz, S. (2021). 8 states debate bills to restrict how teachers discuss racism, sexism. *Education Week.* https://www.edweek.org/policy-politics/8-states-debate-bills -to-restrict-how-teachers-discuss-racism-sexism/2021/04

Stoll, L., Bolam, R., McMahon, A., Wallace, M., & Thomas, S. (2006). Professional learning communities: A review of the literature. *Journal of Educational Change, 7,* 221–258.

Villegas, A. M., & Lucas, T. (2002). Preparing culturally responsive teachers: Rethinking the curriculum. *Journal of Teacher Education, 53*(1), 20–32.

Villegas, A. M., & Lucas, T. (2007). The culturally responsive teacher. *Educational Leadership, 64*(6), 28–33.

Virella, P. (forthcoming). Applying the supervisory behavior continuum to determine a plan of action and support when teaching isn't culturally responsive. In I. M. Mette, D. R. Cormier, & Y. Oliveras-Ortiz (Eds.), *Culturally responsive instructional supervision: Instructional leadership for equitable and emancipatory outcomes.* Teachers College Press.

Waite, S. R. (2021). Towards a theory of critical consciousness: A new direction for the development of instructional and supervisory leaders. *Journal of Educational Supervision, 4*(2), 65–79. https://doi.org/10.31045/jes.4.2.4

Waite, S. R. (forthcoming). The criticality of consciousness in professional development. In I. M. Mette, D. R. Cormier, & Y. Oliveras-Ortiz (Eds.), *Culturally responsive instructional supervision: Instructional leadership for equitable and emancipatory outcomes.* Teachers College Press.

Watson, T. N., & Nash, A. M. (2021). Challenging whiteness at Claremont High School. *Journal of Cases in Educational Leadership, 24*(3), 3–14.

Willey, C., & Magee, P. A. (2019). Whiteness as a barrier to becoming a culturally relevant teacher: Clinical experiences and the role of supervision. *Journal of Educational Supervision, 1*(2), 33–51. https://doi.org/10.31045/jes.1.2.3

Zepeda, S. J. (2016). *Instructional supervision: Applying tools and concepts* (4th ed.). Routledge.

About the Authors

Dr. **Ian M. Mette** is an associate professor of educational leadership and policy at the University at Buffalo. His research interests include teacher supervision, school reform, and how educators, researchers, and policymakers can better inform one another to drive school improvement and reform policy. He is the founding editor of the *Journal of Educational Supervision*, and his first book, *A New Leadership Guide for Democratizing Schools from the Inside Out: The Essential Renewal of America's Schools*, was coauthored with Carl D. Glickman and published in 2020. Dr. Mette holds a PhD in educational administration from the University of Missouri.

Dr. **Dwayne Ray Cormier** is the CEO and founder of Cultural Responsive Solutions, LLC, dedicated to addressing educational sociocultural gaps. Dr. Cormier uses asset-based pedagogical approaches and AI models to illuminate the inequities faced by minoritized, marginalized, and otherized students and families in US PK–12 education. His research focuses on enhancing educators' cultural competence and critical consciousness, improving teacher-student relationships, and fostering positive school culture. Dr. Cormier's research has been published in esteemed journals, including *Educational Researcher, Urban Education, Journal of School Psychology,* and the *Journal of Educational Supervision*. He holds a PhD in curriculum and instruction from The Pennsylvania State University.

Dr. **Yanira Oliveras** is an associate professor and the assistant director of the School of Education at The University of Texas at Tyler. Prior to joining the UT Tyler faculty, she spent 20 years in K–12 education where she served as a teacher, curriculum coordinator, and school principal. Dr. Oliveras's research agenda and service focuses on the advancement of instructional leadership and supervisors in Belize. She is the recipient of a CARSI grant from the US Embassy Belmopan to collaborate with the Belize Ministry of Education. Dr. Oliveras holds a BS in elementary education, MEd, and PhD in curriculum and instruction from The Pennsylvania State University.